In Our Hands

A Peace and Social Justice Program
Junior High

Barry Andrews

Robert C. Branch

Virginia Lane

Harold Rosen

with

Samuel Goldenberg, Eleanor Hunting, Mary Thomson

David Marshak, Developmental Editor

Judith Frediani, Project Editor

A Project of the Peace and Social Justice Curriculum Team

Unitarian Universalist Association

Production Editor: Kathy Wolff
Text Designer: Suzanne Morgan
Cover Designer: Lisa Clark
Editorial Assistant: Timothy Reynolds
Cover Art: Dr. Charlie Clements Peace Quilt © Boise
    Peace Quilt Project. Used by permission.

Acknowledgments

We want to acknowledge the contribution made to the work of the Peace and Social Justice Curriculum Team by Mary Madison during her tenure on the team during 1984-85. We also want to recognize Par Hoertdoerfer's contribution to the final editing of *Junior High*.

We wish to thank all of the Unitarian Universalist young people and adults who took part in the field test, and thus greatly contributed to the development of this program. These field-testers were members of the following congregations: the First Unitarian Universalist Church of Phoenix, Arizona; the Unitarian Church of Vancouver, British Columbia; the North Shore Unitarian Church of North Vancouver, British Columbia; the Jefferson Unitarian Church of Golden, Colorado; the Unitarian Church of Winnipeg, Manitoba; the Unitarian Universalist Church of Silver Spring, Maryland; First Parish of Brewster, Massachusetts; All Souls Church, Unitarian Universalist of Greenfield, Massachusetts; the Unitarian Church of Underwood, Minnesota; the First Unitarian Church of Omaha, Nebraska; the Unitarian Universalist Fellowship of Corvallis, Oregon; the Unitarian Church of Spokane, Washington; East Shore Unitarian Church of Bellevue, Washington; the Bellingham Unitarian Fellowship of Bellingham, Washington; the Michael Servetus Unitarian Fellowship of Vancouver, Washington; and the Northlake Unitarian Universalist Church of Kirkland, Washington. In particular we are grateful for the contribution of Mary Benham of the Unitarian Church of Spokane, who both field-tested the curriculum and critiqued the final draft.

The use of the following material is gratefully acknowledged: "May the Long Time Sun Shine Upon You," reprinted by permission from *The Many Blessings Songbook*. Songbook and cassette tape are available from Spring Hill Music, 5216 Sunshine Canyon, Boulder, CO 80302. Excerpts from *The New Games Book* by Andrew Fluegelman, copyright 1976 by Headlands Press, Inc. Used by permission of Doubleday, a division of Bantam, Dell Publishing Group, Inc. Excerpts from *More New Games* by Andrew Fluegelman, copyright 1981 by Headlands Press, Inc. Used by permission of Doubleday, Dell Publishing Group, Inc. "Common Beliefs" in Session 5 adapted from *World Hunger: Twelve Myths* by Frances Moore Lappe and Joseph Collins (New York: Grove Press, 1986). Reprinted with permission from the Institute for Food and Development Policy, 145 Ninth St., San Francisco, CA 94103. Thanks to Thomas Mikelson for "Susan B. Anthony," printed here with permission. We are also grateful for "The Night Thoreau Spent in Jail," by Jerome Lawrence and Robert E. Lee.

Finally, we wish to acknowledge the contributions made to the development of *Junior High* by the members of the UUA Religious Education Advisory Committee and the Department of Religious Education.

Contents

Introduction to *In Our Hands*

"We, the member congregations of the Unitarian Universalist Association, covenant to affirm and promote the inherent worth and dignity of every person; justice, equity, and compassion in human relations...."

So begins the Principles and Purposes covenant adopted by the Unitarian Universalist Association in 1985. The statement underscores the denomination's deep commitment to justice, a commitment that marks the history of the two liberal religious traditions, Unitarianism and Universalism.

Unitarian Universalists celebrate and remember a worthy collection of forebears who struggled for peace and justice. We remember Benjamin Rush and his timely defense of social equality in the late eighteenth century. We remember Theodore Parker's passion for abolition a generation later. We celebrate Adin Ballou's powerful critique of industrial society, Clara Barton, founder of the American Red Cross, and William Ellery Channing's abhorrence of poverty. We remember Dorothea Dix, reformer of prisons and psychiatric hospitals, and Susan B. Anthony, eminently successful suffragist. We honor Olympia Brown, Jane Addams, Elizabeth Blackwell, and Albert Schweitzer.

In more recent history, we celebrate the contributions of John Haynes Holmes, pacifist, human rights advocate, and co-founder of the War Resister's League and the American Civil Liberties Union. And Donald Thompson, shot as he stood up for civil rights in Jackson, Mississippi, in the early 1960s. We remember James Reeb, beaten to death for the same cause on the streets of Selma, Alabama in 1965 and Whitney Young, Jr. , head of the National Urban League. We celebrate, too, the Unitarian Universalist Association's decision to publish the controversial Pentagon Papers despite government harassment, and the Association's long-standing commitment to gay and lesbian civil rights.

We celebrated the Unitarian Universalist Service Committee's fiftieth anniversary in 1989. The UUSC has worked at home to fund minority-directed community projects, and abroad to enable people to gain control over their political, economic, and social institutions. The UUSC has sponsored many fact-finding missions to Central America to publicize human rights violations. The UUSC has its roots in the Unitarian and Universalist service committees that aided World War II refugees and led humanitarian efforts throughout the world.

Grounded in this rich history, present-day Unitarian Universalists have a commitment to peace and justice that must look forward, not back. With the inspiration of such activists, we must live our lives as peacemakers and champions of fair play.

In Our Hands is a manifestation of our belief in ourselves, our children, and our future. The Peace and Social Justice Curriculum Team began its work in November 1983 and finished in November 1988. The team, consisting primarily of Unitarian Universalists from the Pacific Northwest of the United States and British Columbia, Canada, developed five religious education curricula: programs for children from five to nine years old, from nine to twelve years, for junior-high age, for senior-high age, and for adults.

The team articulated the following statement, which has served as the philosophical center in the development of these curricula.

Peace and Social Justice Education for Unitarian Universalists: A Rationale

The Present Crisis

The most serious issues facing the world today are issues of peace and justice. The nuclear arms race, tyranny, hunger, poverty, torture, terrorism, even pollution and depletion of the world's resources are all problems of peace and justice. At the same time, although the magnitude and urgency of these problems is unprecedented in human history, issues of peace and justice have always been central concerns of human beings.

Linking Peace and Justice

Peace and justice are necessarily interdependent. Each requires the other. Real peace is not possible without justice. Injustice is the result of violence, which is often institutionalized as exploitation and oppression. Injustice is also a cause of violence in the form of criminal behavior, rebellion, and in reprisal, repression. In addition, true justice is not possible without peace. As long as individuals or groups are engaged in threats or acts of aggression, others are deprived of basic human rights, including freedom, equality, and life itself. Thus, peace and justice are both integral to the definition of the other. Peace is the achieving of justice, cooperation, and nonviolence. Justice is the realization of peace, freedom, and equality. Both peace and justice are necessary conditions for human fulfillment.

Ends and Means, Ideals and Realities

Peace and justice are at once ideal goals and actual processes. The vision of a just and peaceful world offers a stimulus for action and a standard by which to judge our efforts. As an actual process, however, peace and justice are always partial and never complete realizations of the ideal goal. Peace and justice are integral parts of the process by which the goals are sought. The means for achieving peace and justice must be congruent with the ends of peace and justice.

Moreover, even as ideal goals, peace and justice must not be viewed as states of perfect accord. A just and peaceful world will not be without disagreement and conflict or the exercise of power. The realization of peace and justice thus requires the nonviolent resolution of disagreement and conflict. It also requires an exercise of power by individuals and institutions that is characterized by and in the service of the ideals of peace and justice.

Cherishing the Earth

Peace and justice include an ecological dimension. The earth is our only source of material sustenance, as well as a major source of our spiritual nurturance. Degradation and destruction of the earth are inherently violent and lead to increasing conflict and injustice. Peace and justice require a reverence for the earth and an understanding of human interdependence, both material and spiritual, with the rest of nature.

Defining Peace and Justice

As an ideal goal, peace and justice are characterized by a set of relationships that describe both absence and presence:

- The *absence* of uncontrolled violence within the individual's psyche; and the *presence* of a sense of wholeness, self-worth, and empowerment within the individual's psyche; the acceptance of inner conflict and the ability to work with such conflict toward growth and integration.
- The *absence* of interpersonal violence; and the *presence* of interpersonal justice, in which justice is defined as fairness and respect due to each person by right and is based upon nonviolence, effective communication, conflict resolution, and cooperation; and the presence of basic political rights, such as freedom and equality, and basic social and economic rights, such as food, health care, employment, and education.
- The *absence* of violence among people of different nations, religions, and cultures; and the *presence* of justice among people of different nations, religions, and cultures, based upon nonviolence, effective communication, conflict resolution, and cooperation.
- The *absence* of destruction of the natural environment; and the *presence* of reverence for nature, and human behavior guided by both this reverence and an understanding of our status as a part of nature and our interdependence with the rest of the natural world.

The ideal of peace and justice is dependent on four kinds of interrelated relationships:
- among the various parts of the individual's psyche (intrapersonal)
- between and among people (intrapersonal)
- between and among institutions of governance and religious faith (inter-institutional)
- between each individual and nature (global).

As we consider peace and justice as a process, not an ideal goal, we must see these characteristics not in terms of absolutes but in terms of their relative absence or presence.

Peace and Justice Education

The objective of peace and justice education is peace- and justice-making (or peacemaking and justice-building). It engages people to stimulate and encourage their development as makers of peace and justice: within their own psyches, in their relationships with others, in their roles as citizens of a nation and members of a religious group, and in their identification as humans living on the earth.

Sources of Authority

Unitarian Universalists derive their authority for peace- and justice-making from several sources:

- their individual commitments to helping create peace and justice on this planet
- their reverence for life
- the Principles and Purposes of the Unitarian Universalist Association, adopted in 1985:

    — The inherent worth and dignity of every person
    — Justice and equity in human relations
    — Democracy and the rights of conscience in our congregations and in society
    — The goal of world community with peace and justice for all
    — Respect for the interdependent web of all existence of which we are a part.

In Our Hands is a product of our history of commitment to peace and justice over the centuries, as exemplified by Unitarian Universalist heroines and heroes, including members of our own congregations and families; and our understanding and appreciation of the world's religions, all of which teach a version of "the golden rule."

Introduction to *Junior High*

In Our Hands: Junior High is a 13-session religious education program for Unitarian Universalist young people in grades seven through nine. (One session is optional.) Each session is planned for one hour.

This program engages participants in exploring their own knowing and feeling about the issues of peace and social justice. First they articulate a vision of a utopian society, one in which peace and justice have been achieved. Then they explore several major phenomena in human life today that manifest conflict and injustice, the opposites of peace and justice: prejudice and "-isms," hunger and poverty, and violence and war. Participants then learn about the contributions of many Unitarian Universalists, contemporary and historical, to making peace and building justice in the world. In the last unit, *In Our Hands* involves the young people in working on peace and justice projects and exploring the nature of legal protest and civil disobedience.

Principles and Goals

In Our Hands is centered on five of the Principles and Purposes adopted by the Unitarian Universalist Association in 1985, as follows:

We, the member congregations of the Unitarian Universalist Association, covenant to affirm and promote:
* The inherent worth and dignity of every person
* Justice, equity, and compassion in human relations
* A free and responsible search for truth and meaning
* The right of conscience and the use of the democratic process
* The goal of world community with peace, liberty, and justice for all.

A central goal is to involve participants in learning about, considering, and exploring these principles in forms that are developmentally appropriate for early adolescents. While people of this age are often self-absorbed, they are also becoming increasingly able to think abstractly, to conceive of and be interested in a larger world beyond family and school, and to be concerned about principles and ideals. This program leads young people to explore familiar intrapersonal and interpersonal territory, and to look beyond themselves to interinstitutional and global issues and concerns.

Another program goal is to acquaint participants with the Unitarian Universalist peace and justice story and vision. Learning about this tradition can help young people feel pride in their identity as Unitarian Universalists and inspire them to contribute to this ongoing story and vision themselves.

Nurturing the participants' interest in and willingness to take part in the causes of peace and social justice is a third goal of *In Our Hands*. In the second half of the program, participants explore ways that people work for peace and justice. In Unit Four, they carry out their own peace and justice projects. In age-appropriate ways, this experience helps young people connect what they have learned in this group with events and circumstances of the larger world and encourages them to act in that world for peace and justice.

Structure

Most of the sessions are organized according to the sections described below. The exceptions are Session 12 and the Optional Session.

Gathering: Bringing participants together, establishing a feeling of connection within the group, and playing an active game

Focusing: Presenting the theme of the session to the participants

Reflecting: Engaging the participants in exploring their own knowing and feeling about the theme

Exploring: Engaging the participants in an activity that expands their knowing and feeling about the theme

Integrating: Involving the participants in expressing what they think and feel now about the theme

Closing: Ending the session with a repeated ritual of being together, briefly reflecting, and singing if desired

Leaders

We strongly recommend a pair of co-leaders for this program. Co-leaders provide a richer experience for the participants by giving them two or more adults with whom they can develop positive and trusting relationships.

Co-leadership also provides significant benefits for the adult leaders: The leaders don't feel isolated from the congregation, because they are working together with another adult. The leaders can share with each other and give feedback to each other. Through these interactions, the leaders can help each other grow. They might also develop a friendship! Co-leadership lessens the pressure on any one leader to attend every session. With co-leaders, each leader can miss a session or two during the course of the program without feeling that this will cause a significant disruption for the participants.

Characteristics of Early Adolescents

Young people in grades seven through nine are usually between the ages of 12 and 15. These are the years of early adolescence, when young people grow beyond childhood into the next era of their lives.

Early adolescents are frequently self-conscious, concerned about their physical appearance and their peers' opinions of them. They are apt to be shy and reluctant to enter groups of strangers by themselves. Yet they usually welcome opportunities to interact with others of the same age and to develop a sense of belonging with a group of peers.

Many early adolescents are growing physically more rapidly than at any other time in their lives except for infancy. They are likely to be awkward and restless and to need opportunities to move around. Many early adolescents particularly enjoy active games and other activities that provide an outlet for their restlessness.

Early adolescents tend to be idealistic. Many are either beginning to think abstractly or are already capable of abstract thought. However, young people of this age can be uninterested in or resistant to learning activities that are primarily intellectual.

Early adolescents respond well to adult leaders who treat them with respect as individuals, help them to build friendships with each other, provide opportunities for them to engage in activities that are active and enjoyable, and emphasize their positive achievements as individuals and as a group. Early adolescents are capable of assuming some leadership roles, but will depend on adult leaders to do most of the organizing and coordinating of activities. They like to feel a sense of ownership of their group, but sometimes have difficulty in carrying out the responsibilities related to that ownership.

Early adolescents are most engaged by activities that spark their idealism, involve them in physical, verbal, and aesthetic activity, and help them to make sense of their own understandings and feelings. They do not respond well to long presentations by a leader or to situations that put them on the spot in front of a group.

In Our Hands: Junior High and Early Adolescence

In Our Hands is a religious education program intended to engage young people intellectually as well as emotionally, interpersonally, aesthetically, and physically. Indeed, of these elements, the intellectual is probably the strongest one in the program.

Some of the activities focus on the early adolescents' common preference for the concrete and their desire to find immediate, personal meaning in all experience. Yet other activities encourage the young people to draw on and develop their emerging potential to think abstractly, to conceive of and be interested in a larger world beyond immediate personal meaning, and to be concerned about principles and ideals.

Of course, there is an inherent tension between these two directions. Encourage participants to take part fully in the activities that tend to stretch and develop their capacities for thinking abstractly and feeling empathetically. At the same time, be attentive to expressions of resistance to these activities. Some resistance is inevitable and probably desirable. Too much is counterproductive. If you encounter too much resistance, feel free to modify the activity in an appropriate direction and/or move along to the next activity in the session sooner than you had planned.

In sum, challenge the young people to employ all of their potentials, yet always be sensitive to their inability and/or unwillingness to do so in any given situation.

Sharing

Inform participants in the very first session that when you invite them to share within this group, it is always their choice to speak or pass, and that passing is okay. Remind people of this option whenever it is appropriate.

Establishing this norm helps young people feel more comfortable in the group, because they will not feel any pressure from you to perform or to reveal anything that they do not choose to share.

Environment

It is important to have a meeting space that is large enough to accommodate the number of young people in your group for the variety of activities in this program.

Have a space that is clean, bright, and aesthetically pleasing. If the space available does not meet these criteria, use imagination and effort to transform it. Enlist the participants and, if desired, some of their parents to work with you. With the involvement of the participants, gather paint, bright fabrics, colorful posters, and cleaning supplies. First have your crew clean the space, and then decorate it. Both you and the young people in your group will appreciate an environment that has been decorated with care and energy.

You will need the following equipment and areas within your space:
- chairs and/or cushions for participants and leaders to sit in a circle
- work tables and chairs for writing and art projects
- wall space for posting banners, signs, and so on
- open floor space for games.

Approximate Times

Each activity is accompanied by an approximate time, which is usually a range. These times are intended to give you information about how long the various activities require for successful enactment. Of course, the actual time required will vary considerably depending on group size, the characteristics of a group, and leadership style. The stated times are suggestions and approximations, not requirements or limitations of any kind.

Preparation Tips

It is important to familiarize yourself with the entire program before beginning. Each week, try to look at least a few sessions ahead so that you are aware of any special preparations that need extra time or coordination.

One way to prepare to lead sessions follows:
1. Read over the session plan.
2. Read it again, jotting down the names of activities and brief descriptions of each on a notecard. You may also want to copy the reading for the Closing.
3. Do the preparation needed for the session.
4. Use the notecard you have prepared to guide you as you lead the session's activities.

Active Games

Most of the Gathering activities include an active game. In the context of a gathering, plan to play the game for five or six minutes.

Some of the purposes of these games are:
- to encourage participants to get to know each other better and be comfortable with each other
- to give participants an opportunity to move around and expend energy at the start of each session, so they can better concentrate on the activities that follow
- to have fun.

Many active games are included in the Index to Games. Choose activities from this list or use other appropriate games that you know.

Closing

Each session in *Junior High* concludes with a Closing. Each Closing includes a chalice lighting, some words relating to peace and justice elements in the UUA Principles and Purposes, and a few moments of silence.

If your group is open to singing together, include a song in the Closing. Choose a song from the Index to Music or from the suggestions of the group. You may want to use a song repeatedly, at least for several weeks, before moving to a new song.

Using the "Reflection and Planning" Questions

At the end of each session plan is a section entitled Reflection and Planning. These questions are designed to guide your reflection about and evaluation of that session. Take the time each week to consider these questions and to discuss them with your co-leader(s). Your deliberate evaluation of your own leadership experience is the best way for you to recognize your leadership strengths and weaknesses, and, working from this recognition, to grow and evolve as a leader. Discussing these questions with your co-leader can provide you with information that you do not perceive, and you can offer similar information to your co-leader.

Even five or 10 minutes of reflection and discussion after each session can make a significant contribution to your growth as a leader. We urge you to make a commitment to this activity.

Informing Parents

Here are some suggestions for informing parents about the *Junior High* program:

- Before the program starts, send a letter to parents describing the goals and activities of *In Our Hands: Junior High*. Invite them to discuss the theme and activities with their young people.
- Early in the program, hold a parents' meeting — during the coffee hour or at night — to discuss this program and its meanings and implications.

"Young Peacemakers" Video

An excellent new video to inspire young people to action is *Young Peacemakers* (EcuFilm, 1989, 20 minutes). This video helps young people see that peace is much more than the absence of war, and that they can have a positive effect on social change. The device of a video game introduces the stories of three teenagers who have become active peacemakers in their communities in a variety of ways.

Tonia Hutchinson, a 16-year-old black girl living in suburban St. Louis, is involved in many social activities through Students for Social Responsibility—including recycling and a hunger program. She has also initiated a black history class for children, held in her home.

Angel Perez is a 12-year-old Puerto-Rican boy who lives in one of the most violent and drug-infested areas of Brooklyn. At school he learned techniques of nonviolent conflict resolution and has become a mediator of conflicts whenever he encounters them. He demonstrates this skill of mediation to viewers, and he expresses his conviction that everyone can be a peacemaker regardless of circumstances.

Susan Goldberg is a Jewish girl of 14. She and others began the Los Angeles Students Coalition, which focuses on consciousness-raising and peaceful protests around such issues as homelessness, the grape boycott, and apartheid in South Africa. In the video, we see Susan and the students commemorating the birthday of Martin Luther King, Jr., by demonstrating against the abuse of children through apartheid.

Young Peacemakers can be purchased from EcuFilm, 810 Twelve Ave., South Nashville, Tennessee 37203, or rented from the UUA Audio-Visual Loan Library, 25 Beacon St., Boston, MA 02108-2800, (617) 742-2100.

Unit One ◆ "The Best of All Possible Worlds"

This unit engages participants in exploring their own beliefs about what would constitute a utopia, or ideal society. This envisioning activity is an entry into an ongoing exploration of peace and social justice issues throughout the program.

In the first two sessions, participants envision an ideal society and articulate that vision through a consensual process. In the third session, the young people create a collage that conveys their utopian image through pictures and words.

Move your group through the first two sessions at a pace that is in harmony with the young people's interest in and engagement with these issues. For example, the Exploring activities in both sessions could take more time than has been allotted in the session plans. If your participants want to explore them in more depth, allow them to do so. If not, move along through these activities as indicated. The purpose of these activities is not to achieve a finished product, but to stimulate involvement with the issues. At the same time, it is important to respect the young people's desire to achieve a sense of closure if they express such a need.

Please note that at the end of Session 2, participants decide as a group whether or not to do Session 3. Some groups are eager to create the collage in Session 3 and very much enjoy this experience. Other groups find the collage activity repetitious and are ready to move on to explore new topics. Explain the choice to your group and let them make the decision.

Session 1 ◆ "The Best of All Possible Worlds"

Goals for Participants

- to get to know each other and/or get to know each other better
- to explore their own beliefs and those of their peers about the needs, rights, and duties of people as members of a society.

Overview

This session invites participants to explore the rights, needs, and duties of people in a human society. This exploration leads the groups to articulate their shared vision of utopia in Session 2.

In this session, you present the young people with the following scenario:

Wise alien beings have arrived on earth. In six months, these aliens will transform every human from her or his current age, sex, race, religion, economic status, and so on to another identity that cannot be predicted. The aliens have given your participants the task of designing a utopian society for the earth, without knowing who the participants will be as individuals after the transformation.

This narrative is intended to engage the young people in envisioning a utopia that is truly ideal for all people, not just for one kind of people.

Encourage participants to use their imaginations as they participate in this activity. They may get ridiculous at times in attempts at humor. Help them enjoy this activity while staying focused on their task.

Materials

- Newsprint, markers, masking tape, and an easel
- 4" x 6" notecards, pins, and markers for nametags
- A copy of Handout 1, "Treasure Hunt," for each participant
- Paper
- Pencils or pens
- Tape player
- A chalice, candle, and matches

Preparation

- It is recommended that you prepare a brief audio-tape of the message from the aliens of Intelligencia Maxima. The script appears in the Focusing section. Ask someone, male or female, inside or outside the congregation, to record this message. Playing a tape, rather than reading the script, adds a note of mystery and drama to this simulation game.

- Be familiar with the entire *In Our Hands: Junior High* program so you can describe it to the group in the Focusing.

- Set up a comfortable circle of chairs and/or cushions.

- Set up the easel so it can be seen by everyone sitting in your circle.

- Have wall space available where newsprint sheets can be taped and visible to the group.

- Set up the nametag materials on the table.

- Make a nametag for yourself, and wear it from the beginning of the session.

- Set up the tape player, and cue up the alien tape.

- Choose an active game to play in the Focusing, and be prepared to lead it.

- Notice that item #5 in Handout 1 includes a blank. Fill this in with the name of a comic strip that is popular with your group.

Session Plan

Gathering   10-15 minutes

Put on your nametag. Greet participants individually as they arrive. Introduce yourself to anyone
you do not know.

Direct each participant to the nametag materials
and invite her or him to make a nametag. Ask
people to print their first names in large, peaceful
letters. Encourage them to use whatever colors,
symbols, or images that suggest peace to them.
When the young people have completed their
nametags, have them pin or tape them on.

When the group has gathered and people have
completed their nametags, ask them to join you in
a circle. Introduce yourself. Then engage the
young people in the treasure hunt by saying
something like: "We are going to go on a brief
treasure hunt: for those of us who don't know each
other, to begin to get acquainted; for those of us
who do know each other, to say hello again."

Distribute Handout 1. Then go on: "Here are
the rules. Fill out as many items on the sheet as you
can by asking people for the information. You
cannot use anything you already know about a
person. You have to discover it right now by
asking. When you have learned something that fits
one of these categories, write the person's name on
your sheet. You are done when you have everyone's
name at least once on your sheet."

Emphasize that people need to discover new
information about each other. Invite questions
about the process, then ask the young people to
begin. Be sure to take part yourself. After four to
five minutes, call an end to the hunt.

Gather the group in a circle. Invite reactions to
the treasure hunt. Then ask people to introduce
themselves in another way by completing the
following sentence:

My name is...and I am most peaceful when...

If appropriate, model the process by completing
this sentence first. Then invite the participants to
continue.

Focusing   10-15 minutes

Give the young people a brief overview of the entire
program. Note the major themes and highlights,
and cite examples of some of the most exciting
activities. You may want to jot these down on
newsprint as you note them. Invite questions.

When you have responded to questions about
the program, engage the young people in playing
an active game for about five minutes.

Then gather the group in a circle, and give
participants a brief overview of the remainder of
this session. Say something like: "I am going to tell
you an imaginary story that will become a
simulation that we will play out."

Explain that a simulation means acting out a
situation or scene as if it were real. Go on: "As you
hear this story, use your imagination to feel what it
would be like if it were real. Suppose that tomorrow
the Earth is taken over by wise and peaceful aliens
who have come from somewhere outside this solar
system. The aliens broadcast the following message
on all the TV and radio stations in the world."

Play the tape of the message, whose script is:

"Hello, people of Earth. We have come to your
small planet from a solar system in a galaxy far
away. Our planet is called Intelligencia Maxima.
We have come to save you from destroying
yourselves. We have determined that the best way
to save you is to let you start all over again, keeping
all that you have already learned. In two weeks, we
will cover the Earth with a specially designed Human
Warp Laser Field. This Warp will transform every
person randomly. After the Warp, everyone will be
a different person. There is no way to predict
anything about who you will be in terms of sex, age,
race, intelligence, wealth, size, location of home,
and so on.

"You have two weeks to redesign the society of
the Earth so that everyone can share peace and
justice. Remember: you do not know who you will
be after the Warp. Thus, as you design your society,
you must consider the needs and wants of everyone.

"We suggest that you answer these questions:
What are the basic needs of people? What rights
should be guaranteed for all? What duties should
all have toward society?

"You will have only two weeks to create your
new design. Begin now. We shall contact you in
two weeks."

Invite questions about the situation described
by the story. Continue the discussion until you are
sure that the young people understand the situation.
Ask questions like:

- What has happened?

- What are the aliens going to do?

- What do we have to do?

Exploring   10-20 minutes

Organize participants into groups of three. If necessary, have a group or two with four members. Give each group three sheets of newsprint and a marker. Invite them to brainstorm responses to the three questions asked by the Intelligencia Maximanians.

If the young people are not familiar with brainstorming, explain that it is a process in which you first raise all the ideas you can think of without judging them, knowing that you'll evaluate them later. Emphasize that in brainstorming, you don't argue or even discuss the idea. You just list everything that comes to mind, even if it may seem silly or not useful at first.

Ask the small groups to respond to the first question. Restate the question: "What are the basic needs of people?" Tell the young people that they have four minutes to reply. Ask them to write their responses on a sheet of newsprint. Then have the participants begin.

As the groups work, move from group to group as needed, helping them to stay focused on their task.

After about four minutes, gather the group. Have the small groups take turns sharing a need from their lists while you record the needs on newsprint.

Follow the same process with the rights and the duties questions.

When you have completed this process, explain to the participants that they will use these lists at the next session to help them respond to the Maximanians' challenge.

Integration and Closing   8-10 minutes

Gather the group in a circle. Ask the young people to think about which need they believe to be the single most important one. Go around the circle, asking people to say which need they chose and why. Model this sharing if no one is eager to go first.

If time allows, follow the same procedure with rights and duties.

Then give a brief overview of the next session, highlighting what the participants will perceive as the most interesting activities.

Place the chalice in a central location. Note that you'd like to close each session with a few moments of reflection and some words that speak to the activities of the session. (If you want to include a song in the Closing, note this as well.)

Have a participant light the chalice. Wait a few moments and then say: "As Unitarian Universalists we aspire to peace and justice for all who dwell on the earth."

If you are including a song, lead the group in singing it.

Have someone extinguish the chalice. Then say goodbye.

As the participants leave, collect the nametags to be used again. Also, be sure to save the three lists of needs, rights, and duties created by the group for Session 2.

Reflection and Planning

Consider these questions, and discuss them with your co-leader(s):

1. What was good about this session? Why?

2. What was not so good? Why?

3. What can I learn from this experience that can help me to be a better leader for this group?

4. What preparation do I need to do for the next session?

Session 2 ♦ Building a Utopian Society

Goals for Participants

- to continue to get to know each other better
- to explore their vision of an ideally peaceful and just society—a utopia.

Overview

In this session, participants explore their beliefs about the relative importance of various human needs, rights, and duties and sketch out a vision of a utopian society. The intent of the activities is to involve the young people in considering the issues. It is not necessary for them to create a finished product in this session, unless they wish to do so.

Materials

- Newsprint, markers, masking tape, and an easel
- Sheets of scrap paper
- Pens or pencils
- Nametags from Session 1
- Nametag materials for newcomers
- The group lists of needs, rights, and duties from Session 1
- A chalice, candle, and matches

Preparation

- Set up a circle and the easel as you did for the previous session.

- Post the lists of needs, rights, and duties from the previous session in a prominent place.

- Have the nametag materials available for newcomers.

Session Plan

Gathering   8-10 minutes

Put on your own nametag. Greet the participants individually as they arrive, and ask them to wear their nametags. Greet any newcomers, and invite them to make and wear nametags.

When the group has gathered, ask people to join you in a circle. Introduce the newcomers to the group. Go around the circle, asking each participant to share her or his name and to describe something that happened during the past week that made her or him laugh. You may want to go first to model the process.

Then engage the young people in playing the game 1-2-3-4. Teach the game by saying something like: "I want each of you to hold one of your ears. Now get together with two other people who are holding the same ear that you are. Now stand facing each other, and each of you put out a clenched fist in front of yourself. Bounce your fists up and down as you chant together, "One, two, three, four." That's all you can say in this whole game. On the count of four, each of you will put out any number of fingers from the hand you have in the middle. The object of the game is to have the number of fingers on all three hands add up to 11, without talking."

If you have one extra person, have a group of four, and tell that group they have to get 13. If you have two extras, join them as a group.

Once the groups have achieved 11, have them try to get 23 using both hands.

Play the game quickly for three or four minutes.

Focusing   5 minutes

Gather participants in a circle, and give them a brief overview of this session.

Exploring   12-20 minutes

Tell the young people that you are going to return to the simulation introduced at the last session. Elicit from them a description of the circumstances and events of the simulation. Be sure that these events are clearly understood by any newcomers. Then hand out a sheet of scrap paper and a pen or pencil to each participant.

Note that for people to design an ideal society, they need to know which needs must be fulfilled, which rights must be honored, and which duties must be accepted. Draw the participants' attention to the list of needs compiled by the whole group last session. Ask them to consider the items on the list, and decide which three needs are the most important. Give them a minute or two to decide and write down their choices on scrap paper. Then have a volunteer share his or her list. Write these needs on a sheet of newsprint. Continue with this procedure until all have shared. When a particular need is cited more than once, put a checkmark next to it for each additional citation.

When all have shared, circle the five most cited needs, and invite comments or questions about the selection of these needs as the most important ones.

Follow this procedure with the lists of rights and duties.

Integrating   20-25 minutes

If participants are restless, engage them in playing an active game for a few minutes before starting this activity.

Begin this activity by saying something like: "Now it's up to us to redesign society. That's the task the Maximanians have given to us. How can we redesign society so that people's needs and rights are guaranteed, and their duties are clear and fair?"

Divide the group into small groups of three or four, and give each small group a sheet of newsprint and a marker. Explain that you'd like each small group to discuss what would make an ideal society, and to describe briefly that society. Ask the participants to keep in mind the needs, rights, and duties that the whole group has determined are most important. List the following terms on a sheet of newsprint: individual, society, nature, technology. Invite the young people to use these terms as a way to organize their descriptions of an ideal society. Give an example or two of how this can be done. (For instance, the right to vote may go under individual; protection of endangered species may go under nature.)

Invite questions about the task, and respond to them as needed. Then have the small groups begin. Move from group to group, answering questions and providing assistance as needed.

Tell the participants when they have only five minutes left for their group work. Ask them to write on newsprint any agreements they have reached about an ideal society.

When time requires, gather the young people in a circle, and have each small group present its description of an ideal society. When all groups have presented, ask the participants to identify the elements of an ideal society that appear most often on the lists. Invite questions and comments.

Before you conclude this activity, ask people if they know what the word "utopia" means. Be sure that everyone understands that a utopia is an ideal human society.

Closing   4-6 minutes

Describe the collage activity in Session 3. Ask the group if they wish to do this activity or omit it. If the group chooses to omit Session 3, give a brief preview of Session 4.

Place the chalice in the center of the group and have a participant light it. Say something like: "As Unitarian Universalists we accept one another — our various insights, our many visions. May this flame be a symbol of our belief in the value of ourselves and each other."

Allow a few moments of silence. If you usually sing a song, do so now. Then have a participant extinguish the flame. Say goodbye.

Collect the nametags as people leave. Save the lists of the five most important needs, rights, and duties and the small group descriptions of an ideal society.

Reflection and Planning

Consider these questions, and discuss them with your co-leader(s):

1. How do I feel about this session?

2. If I were going to lead this session again, what would I change about it? Why?

3. Do any participants indicate a need for special attention from me? If so, who and what kind of attention?

4. What preparation do I need to do for the next session?

Session 3 ◆ Promoting Our Utopian Society

Goals for Participants

- to continue to get to know each other better
- to understand the concept of utopia and their vision of a utopian society.

Overview

In this session the young people design and create a collage that illustrates their vision of a utopia. This activity helps them deepen their understanding of their own and their peers' ideas about an ideal society and involves them in an enjoyable, cooperative enterprise.

If the group has 10 or more members, consider splitting into two small groups and have each small group make its own collage.

Materials

- Tagboard or posterboard at least 3' x 4'
- Scissors (include left-handed)
- Glue

- Many pictorial magazines, such as *National Geographic, Sunset Nature, Ranger Rick, Life, Equinox, Discovery, Science,* and *Smithsonian*
- Many newspapers and news magazines
- Nametags from previous sessions
- Nametag materials for newcomers
- A chalice, candle, and matches

Preparation

- Set up your usual circle.

- Post in prominent locations the lists of the five most important needs, rights, and duties and the small group descriptions of an ideal society.

- Set up work tables and chairs.

- Gather a variety of magazines and newspapers that represent cultural and racial diversity as well as the natural world. Place them with the scissors and glue on the tables.

- Print the four headings on the tagboard as shown in the diagram:

Nature		Individual
A		
	C	B
Society		Technology

- Note that in the structure of the collage, pictures and words placed closest to a heading are to relate exclusively to that term as it applies to the utopia. Pictures and words placed equidistant between two headings are to relate to both of those terms. Pictures and words placed in the center of the collage are to relate to all four headings. For example, items placed near A on the diagram would relate to nature in the utopia. Items placed near B would relate to the interaction between the individual and technology in the utopia. Items placed near C would relate to all headings.

Session Plan

Gathering   5-10 minutes

Greet participants as they arrive. Hand out the nametags, and ask people to wear them. Invite newcomers to make and wear nametags.

When the group has gathered, ask people to sit in a circle. If participants are still learning each others' names, engage them in playing the Name Game. If they already know each others' names, play an active game.

Name Game

Ask people to remove their nametags temporarily. Then play the following game:

The first person introduces herself or himself in the following way: "My name is Sam, and I like sailing." The introduction consists of the first name and something the person likes beginning with the same letter as his or her name. The person to the first person's right must repeat the first introduction and then give his or her own introduction in the same manner. The third person repeats the first two introductions and his or her own, and so on. Continue until all participants and leaders have had a turn. If people get lost, help them out so they are not embarrassed.

Focusing   3-5 minutes

Give people a brief overview of this session. Have participants quickly review the story of the Intelligencia Maximanians and your group's response so far.

Exploring   10-12 minutes

Draw the participants' attention to the small group descriptions of an ideal society that are posted. Invite them to identify elements of a utopia that appear in two or more of the descriptions.

Print "Utopia" on a sheet of newsprint, and list the elements that appear in more than one small group description.

Help participants see these elements as part of a consensual description of an ideal society, a vision shared by many members in the group. As time allows, invite discussion.

If there are no common elements among the descriptions, use this time to help the young people reach some agreements about what constitutes an ideal society.

The goal of this activity is to move toward a rough consensus about the nature of utopia. It is not expected that the group will achieve a complete consensus in the time available. Allot only 10-12 minutes to this effort, so you will have adequate time for the collage.

Integrating   25-35 minutes

Explain that you will now ask the group to illustrate what their ideal society would be like by creating a collage that depicts a utopia. If the group wishes, you can display the finished collage in an appropriate place in the congregation's building. Note that the group can decide this later.

Post the tagboard you have prepared, and explain the structure of the collage. Be sure that people understand that they are to use both pictures and words on the collage. Invite questions about the collage-making process.

When everyone understands the concept of the collage, offer the following ground rules:

- Everyone shares the materials: magazines, news-papers, scissors, and glue.

- Before you can attach anything to the collage, you need to get one other person to agree that what you want to attach is appropriate.

When everyone understands the ground rules, invite them to begin. If desired, play a tape of peace and justice songs as the group works.

If disputes arise about the appropriateness of an item, intervene quickly. Have those for and against state their positions briefly. Then call for a vote, with majority rule.

Let people know when they have only five more minutes to work on the collage.

Closing   7-10 minutes

Gather the participants in a semicircle in front of the collage. Engage them in discussing and responding to the following questions:

1. Does the collage effectively represent our ideal society? (If it does not, consider how the group can make it represent their vision of a utopia more effectively. Decide on a plan for achieving this.)

2. What title should we put on the collage? (When the group selects a title, have a volunteer create it and attach it to the collage.)

Ask the group if they'd like to display the collage to the congregation. If they do, make arrangements after this session.

When time requires, place the chalice in the center of the semicircle. Give a brief preview of the next session. Then have a participant light the chalice. Say, "As Unitarian Universalists we believe in the ongoing search for truth and meaning. May this flame inspire us to share our truths with each other and with other people in our lives. "

Allow a few moments of silence. If you are using a song, sing it now.

Have a participant extinguish the chalice. Say goodbye to the young people.

Note: Depending on how well the young people in the group know each other, decide if you want to use nametags after this session.

Reflection and Planning

Consider these questions, and discuss them with your co-leader(s):

1. What did I like most about this session? Why?

2. What did I like least? Why?

3. What preparation do I need to do for the next session?

Unit Two ◆ What About...?

In Unit One, participants explored their own beliefs about what would constitute a utopian society. This unit engages the young people in considering three of the major forms of injustice and violence in the world: prejudice and "-isms," hunger and poverty, and interpersonal violence and war. The prevalence of these social conditions throughout the planet makes the reality of human life vastly different from any vision of utopia. Each of these forms of violence and injustice is explored in relation to the young people's life experience.

The purposes of this unit are:
- to help participants gain a wider understanding of the nature of injustice and violence in the world
- to involve participants in learning more about what limits and blocks the creation of more peaceful and just conditions in the world
- to allow participants to get in touch with their own feelings and understandings in relation to injustice and violence in their own lives.

Please note that in this unit participants receive an envelope or folder for their handouts. It is recommended that these be kept in the meeting space until the end of the program. The folders are described in detail in Session 4.

Session 4 ◆ What About Prejudice and "-Isms"?

Goals for Participants

- to explore their own experience with prejudice, stereotyping, and "-isms"
- to develop a deeper understanding of these concepts and their implications
- to become more aware of their own prejudices and stereotypes.

Overview

Prejudice and stereotyping are among the root causes of much injustice and conflict in our society and throughout the world. One intent of this session is to help participants learn what prejudice, stereotyping, and various "-isms" are, and to have them consider the implications of these attitudes and values in their own lives. A second purpose is to encourage participants to feel empathy for those who suffer from prejudice and "-isms," and to develop a greater appreciation for the value of human diversity.

Use the following definitions in this session:

A prejudice is an unfavorable attitude toward, feeling about, or opinion of a person or group of persons based on ignorance and/or misinformation.

A stereotype is a generalization about a group of people that is founded in ignorance or misinformation.

For example, if a person says that he doesn't like French people because they are arrogant, he is indicating both a belief in a stereotype that all French people are arrogant, and a prejudicial attitude that he doesn't like all French people based on that stereotype.

An "-ism" is a consequence of prejudice embedded in institutional actions. When people with institutional power hold prejudices, they cause the institutions to generate prejudicial outcomes. Yet institutions can create prejudicial outcomes even when the people in power are not consciously prejudiced. These outcomes result from the fact that institutions have a life and a momentum of their own, a force that is difficult for individuals to change.

An example of an "-ism" is racism. When people who hold prejudices against persons of color wield power in an institution, the outcomes of that institutional action are racist. Yet institutions run by people who are not consciously prejudiced against people of color can also generate racist outcomes.

For your participants, define "-ism" as follows: An "-ism" results when prejudiced people have power over people they are prejudiced against. A shorthand is the following: prejudice plus power = "-isms."

Materials

- Newsprint, markers, and tape
- A sheet of white cardboard or oaktag for every two participants
- Markers, poster paints, and other drawing and coloring media
- 9" x 12" envelope or folder for each participant
- A chalice, candle, and matches

Preparation

- Obtain 9" x 12" manila folders or envelopes for the young people.

- Set up your usual circle.

- Have work tables available for decorating folders and making posters, and place the art materials on the tables.

- Print the definitions of prejudice, stereotyping, and "-isms" on a sheet of newsprint to be posted during the Exploring.

Session Plan

Gathering   10-15 minutes

Greet participants as they arrive. Hand out the folders or envelopes, and explain their purpose (to keep all of the handouts they will receive in this program.) Ask the young people to write their names on the folders and invite them to personalize their folders by decorating them with the drawing and coloring material provided. Suggest that they portray one or more elements of their own utopia on the covers. Note that they can keep the folders in their meeting space until the end of the program.

When the group has gathered and participants have decorated their folders or envelopes, ask people to join you in the circle. Invite participants to share one good thing that happened to them in the past week. You may want to go first to model this sharing.

When all have shared who wish to do so, engage the group in playing an active game.

After the game, gather the group in a circle. Briefly review what the group has done so far in this program and provide a quick introduction to Unit Two that includes a transition from Unit One. Then give a brief overview of this session.

Focusing   3 minutes

Invite participants to suggest the names for types of people in their school. As people suggest a type, list it on a sheet of newsprint.

Reflecting   6-9 minutes

When participants have offered all of their suggestions of types, pick one — if possible, the one that has the most negative associations attached to it — and engage the young people in responding to the questions below in relation to that type:

• What is a _____?

• How do you know one when you see one?

• Are they worthy of our acquaintance?

• Would you be seen in public with one?

• Would you have one as a friend?

• Are there times when you act like one of these types?

Without preaching, encourage participants to discover and articulate the ways in which this type is a label that is unjust to anyone to whom we apply it.

Exploring   12-18 minutes

Explain that this type is a stereotype. Invite participants to define stereotype. If they can do so, confirm the accuracy of their definition as you post the definitions sheet that you have prepared.

If the participants cannot define stereotype, post the definitions sheet and share the definition with them.

In either case, ask the group to offer other examples of stereotyping.

Go over the definitions of prejudice and "-isms" with the group. Then ask: What are some examples of prejudice? Of "-isms"? Invite responses.

Help the young people to understand the differences among these three terms.

Organize the group into smaller groups of three. Say something like: "There are many ways that we judge and label people unfairly and then treat them unjustly based on these judgments. As we have already seen, quite often these judgments are based on outward appearances, such as clothes, color of skin, sex, and so on. Have you ever been labeled by other people in a way that you felt was unfair?"

Invite participants to share their responses to this question with their partners. Ask them to consider the following questions in their discussion:

• What happened?

• How did you feel when you were treated this way?

• How do you think the person who treated you unfairly felt?

When people have shared, gather the whole group in a circle. Invite people to share any questions or comments they have about prejudice, stereotyping, and "-isms."

Integrating   15-20 minutes

Have the young people organize into pairs. Give each pair a sheet of cardboard or tagboard. Invite each pair to make a poster that conveys a message about prejudice and/or stereotyping. Invite questions about the project. Then have the participants move to the work tables where the markers and paints are available. Invite them to begin their posters. Be available for help and encouragement as needed. You may want to play a tape of peace and justice songs while the young people work.

Let participants know when they have five minutes left. If people want more time to work on their posters, schedule the additional time in a way that is appropriate for your group.

Closing   6-9 minutes

When the participants have completed their posters, have them post them on a wall for display. Invite people to look at each other's posters.

Gather the group in a circle, and invite reactions to the display of posters. Ask participants if they would like to display their posters for your congregation. If so, make appropriate arrangements after this session.

If participants have not completed their posters, defer the above sharing until they have finished. In either case, conclude with the following activity.

Give the young people a brief preview of the next session. Then place the chalice in the center of your circle, and have a participant light it. Ask the participants to close their eyes and keep them closed until you ask them to open them again. Then say something like: "We all have prejudices and stereotypes inside us. But we can become more and more aware of them, and we can learn to let them go."

Share one prejudice or stereotype that you have held at some point in your life that you have grown beyond. Then say:

"I'd like you to think of one prejudice or stereotype that you hold now that you'd like to get rid of." (Pause for 10 seconds.) "And now I'd like you to imagine yourself taking that prejudice or stereotype and throwing it away from you with all of your might." (Pause for 10 seconds.) "And now you are free from that prejudice or stereotype, and it won't influence you ever again." (Pause for five seconds.)

Ask the young people to open their eyes and look into the flame of the chalice. Then say:
"As Unitarian Universalists we believe in the worth and dignity of all people — their thoughts and feelings, their beliefs, and their dreams. May this flame help us to remember that every single person is important."

Allow a few seconds for reflection. If desired, lead the group in a song. Then have a participant extinguish the flame. Say goodbye.

If possible, display the posters in your space for the rest of the program.

Reflection and Planning

Consider these questions, and discuss them with your co-leader(s):

1. What have you learned from the experience of this session?

2. Do I want to change the way I interact with any of the young people? If so, why and how?

3. What preparations do I need to do for the next session?

Session 5 ♦ What About Hunger and Poverty?

Goals for Participants

- to experience through simulation the unequal distribution of the world's food resources
- to increase their understanding of the unequal distribution of the world's food resources and the consequences of this distribution
- to explore the causes and effects of hunger among the people of the world
- to consider possible solutions to this problem.

Overview

Participants are not likely to know much about the causes or effects of hunger in the world. Their impressions regarding this problem have been shaped, as indeed most of ours have, by images of starving masses of people on television news. While indisputably real, these images are misleading. Although any number of causes of hunger have been suggested, including drought, overpopulation, and lack of technological development, the truth of the matter is that poverty is the major cause of hunger. It is not the rich who are hungry or starving; it is the poor.

This session makes participants more aware of the realities of hunger and poverty in the world. The young people are introduced to basic information about this situation and to a clarification of some misconceptions about hunger and the food supply. Participants also explore possible solutions to the problem.

It is recommended that you learn more about the issue of hunger before you lead this session. One source of information is the Church World Service. If this organization does not have an office in your area, write to the national office at P.O. Box 968, Elkhart, IN 46515. An excellent introduction to the topic is *World Hunger: Twelve Myths* by Frances Moore Lappe and Joseph Collins (San Francisco: Institute for Food Development Policy, 1984). Your congregation may have a copy.

Materials are also available from the Unitarian Universalist Service Committee at 78 Beacon St., Boston, MA 02108.

For your information, a fact sheet on world hunger is included in this session.

Please note that the map used in the handout "Hunger — A World Divided" is the Peters projection, which shows more accurately the actual proportions of land surface areas than does the more familiar Mercator projection. In the Peters projection, commisioned by the United Nations, every square unit of map surface represents an equal square unit of land surface. The Mercator projection overemphasizes the Northern Hemisphere (Europe and the United States) at the expense of the Southern Hemisphere (South America, Africa, and the Indian subcontinent.) Participants may comment that the Peters projection looks odd. Explain that any two-dimensional representation of Earth, a sphere, will be distorted in some way, but that the Peters projection shows how big different countries and continents really are compared with one another.

To order a Peters projection wall map, contact Friendship Press, P.O. Box 37844, Cincinnati, OH 45237 or your local bookstore.

Materials

- Materials for the simulation "How the World Eats," which is located at the end of this session
- Copies of Handout 2, "Hunger — A World Divided"
- Pens or pencils
- Five copies of "Common Beliefs," located in this session
- Newsprint
- A chalice, candle, and matches

Preparation

- Set up your circle as usual.

- Set up the table for the simulation "How the World Eats." Cover the food with a cloth.

- Print the first sentence in each Common Belief at the top of a sheet of newsprint.

- Familiarize yourself with the issue of hunger as described in the Overview. There may be someone in your congregation who would be a willing resource for you and the group.

Session Plan

Gathering   8-12 minutes

Greet participants as they arrive. When the group has gathered, ask people to join you in a circle.

Invite participants to briefly share something interesting or special that happened to them in the past week. When all have shared who wish to do so, engage them in playing an active game.

Focusing   5-7 minutes

Gather the group. Quickly review the previous session, and give a brief overview of this session. Then engage the participants in the simulation "How the World Eats" (before Session 6).

Please note: As this is not the major activity of this session, move through it quickly.

Reflecting   5-7 minutes

Before discussing the simulation, tell the participants that the treats will be equally divided at snack time. For now, leave the set-up as it is.

Engage the young people in discussing the simulation by asking questions like:

- How do you feel about what the others got compared to what you got?

- How do you think the others feel about what they got?

- Is it just (or fair) that the others received more or less than you did?

- Why do you think the world's food and other resources are distributed the way they are?

Exploring   25-35 minutes

Distribute copies of Handout 2 and the pens or pencils. Introduce this activity by saying something like the following:

"Let's take a look now at another plate, this one with a map of the world on it. It's a cracked plate. The crack represents the divisions between the rich and the poor nations of the world. Below the plate are a few questions for you to answer."

Explain the Peters projection map used in this handout as described in Overview. Ask the young people to complete the questions in "Hunger—A World Divided." When they have finished, go over the questions and discuss the answers given here:

Answers

1. (d) One billion

2. (d) 13,000,000

3. (d) 3/4

4. (b) 17%

5. (c) 50

6. (a) 3%

As appropriate, share information from the "World Hunger Fact Sheet," located at the end of this session. Guide the discussion to exploring the causes of and possible solutions to the problem of hunger in the world.

After some discussion of causes and possible solutions, divide the group into five pairs or small groups. Give each group a sheet of newsprint on which you have written a Common Belief. Explain that the Common Belief they have been given might be true or false, and that you would like them to discuss the idea and decide if they think it's true.

After about five minutes, or when they have made decisions, have each group read aloud their belief and then report the decision to the whole group. When all have reported, hand out one copy of "Common Beliefs" to each small group. Have those with Belief #1 read aloud the commentary about this myth. Invite discussion. Be sure that participants understand that the commentary represents the views of Frances Moore Lappe and Joseph Collins, two experts on world food supply and hunger.

Follow the same procedure with the other beliefs.

If you have fewer than 10 participants in your group, create as many pairs as you can. Give each pair a Common Belief to discuss and follow the procedure described above. Then present any unexamined Common Beliefs to the group after the pairs have reported, and engage them in a discussion of these ideas.

Integrating   5-10 minutes

Ask the young people how hunger might be lessened in the world. Encourage responses. If appropriate, bring the discussion to a consideration of what, if anything, the young people feel they can do themselves about helping to alleviate hunger. Consider asking:

What can we do as a group that might help people get the food they need?

Be open to the possibility that the group will want to engage in a social service activity related to this, for example, fund-raising for a food bank, participating in a walk against hunger, and so on.

Closing   6-9 minutes

Redistribute the treats fairly, and invite everyone to have a snack. Discussion may continue while you eat.

When the group has finished the snack, gather the group in a circle. Give them a brief preview of the next session. Then place the chalice in the center of the circle, and have a participant light it. Say, "As Unitarian Universalists, we affirm compassion for those in need, and our responsibility to help those who have less than we do. May this flame inspire us to find ways to share the good things in life more fairly."

Allow a few moments of silence. If the group wants to, lead them in singing a song. Then have a participant extinguish the chalice.

Say goodbye to the participants.

Reflection and Planning

Consider these questions, and discuss them with your co-leader(s):

1. If I were leading this session again, how would I change it?

2. What is the overall quality of the feeling among the young people in the group? Are there any interpersonal issues that I'd like to address in any way?

3. What preparation do I need to do for the next session?

Common Beliefs

1. There is not enough food and not enough land to grow food for all the people on the Earth.

   Not true! There is land to grow enough food to feed everyone. The problem is that some people can afford to buy more food than they need while others do not have enough, because they are too poor to pay for it. Also, many rich people who own good land grow crops for money rather than food to feed poor people.

2. There are too many people to feed.

   No, there is enough food for everyone right now. But many people around the world are too poor to buy the food they need. These poor people often have many children, because they hope their children will be able to get jobs and help to earn money for food. In this way, hunger often leads to an increasing number of people.

3. Growing more food will mean less hunger in poor countries.

   No, the truth is that most of the land in poor countries is owned by a few wealthy people, not by poor people. Much of the food grown in poor countries is shipped away and sold in the U.S., Canada, and elsewhere, so the wealthy landowners can earn money for it.

4. Hunger is a contest between rich countries and poor countries.

   No, we are all part of the same world food system, and we are all neighbors on this planet. There is enough food for all. To feed hungry people, we don't need to deprive ourselves of what we need. But we do need to support people in poor countries gaining control of their own land.

5. Hunger can be solved by giving food to the hungry.

   No, this only helps right now. But what about next month and next year? People will always be hungry if they cannot grow food and are too poor to buy it. Only when poor people own land for growing food or have good jobs will they be safe from hunger.

Adapted from *World Hunger: Twelve Myths*, by Frances Moore Lappe and Joseph Collins (New York: Grove Press, 1986).

World Hunger Fact Sheet

The persistence of world hunger is one of those issues that permeates the background of life. With the exception of the occasional newsmaking event — typically, famine in which the human disaster is so acute that it cannot be ignored — hunger lives as a process, a persistence, a chronic condition. People die day in, day out; and because this is the norm, it is not "news."

For those of us who are adequately fed and for whom food is commonplace in daily life, hunger — if it is thought of at all — is something "out there"; something tragic, horrible, awful; something we wish did not exist. It is not, however, something we keep front and center as one of our primary and fundamental concerns.

Imagine our concern — and the attention of the world's media — were an earthquake to strike San Francisco, killing 35,000 people in a single day.

Imagine our concern were a virus to descend on London, killing 18 children a minute without stop, week after week after week.

Imagine our concern were nuclear weapons to explode in the capitals of the world's major industrial countries, killing 13 million people and maiming and injuring a billion more in the surrounding countryside.

These are precisely the figures of human devastation resulting from hunger: one billion of us chronically undernourished; 13 to 18 million of us dead a year; 35,000 of us a day; 24 of us (18 of whom are children) a minute. Yet because we view hunger in the background of life, this terrible toll does not enter our headlines, nor, for most of us, our concerns...

All of us have been "hungry" at some time or other. This usually means simply that we have an appetite. But the hunger experienced by hundreds of millions of people on our planet is not an appetite that comes and goes: it is a consuming, debilitating, minute-by-minute, day-after-day experience. Hunger — the persistent, chronic, relentless condition — keeps people from working productively and thinking clearly. It decreases their resistance to disease. It can be intensely painful. Prolonged hunger can result in permanent damage to body and mind. And, ultimately, if hunger goes on long enough, it kills...

This intensely dehumanizing and debilitating hunger is experienced by one out of every five people on the planet. The facts are staggering:

• More than one billion people are chronically hungry.

• Every year 13 to 18 million people die as a result of hunger and starvation.

• Every 24 hours, 35,000 human beings die as a result of hunger and starvation — 24 every minute, 18 of whom are children under five years of age.

• No other disaster compares to the devastation of hunger.

• More people have died from hunger in the past two years than were killed in World War I and World War II combined.

• The number of people who die every two days of hunger and starvation is equivalent to the number who were killed instantly by the Hiroshima bomb.

• The worst earthquake in modern history — in China in 1976 — killed 242,000 people. Hunger kills that many people every seven days.

Ending Hunger: An Idea Whose Time Has Come, The Hunger Project (New York: Praeger, 1985), 2, 6-7.

How the World Eats: A Simulation

Objective

- To increase participants' awareness of the food and wealth distribution among First, Second, and Third World countries.

Overview

This activity was adapted from material produced by the Church World Service, Office on Global Education, with the Center for Teaching International Relations at the University of Denver.

The group will be divided into representatives of First, Second, and Third World countries.

For every 10 participants, two represent the First World nations; one the Second World nations; and seven the Third World nations. Actual population figures are: First World, 17%; Second World, 9%; Third World, 74%.

For groups of more or fewer than 10, work out appropriate proportions so everyone participates. Don't worry about achieving exact statistical accuracy, but rather conveying the overall message of unequal distribution of wealth and food.

Materials

- Three menu cards (descriptions follow)
- Twenty treats such as cookies, brownies, rice cakes, bags of raisins
- Cardboard circles to serve as tokens
- A bag for the tokens
- Three plates

Preparation

Tokens

Cardboard circles serve as tokens. For each group of 10, make two tokens with the words "First World" on them, one with the words "Second World," and seven with the words "Third World."

Menu Cards

Make one of each of the following:

Card #1: First World

Canada, France, Japan, Norway, United States, West Germany, and other industrialized countries. You have 17% of the world's population and 56% of the world's wealth. Your share is 11 treats.

Card #2: Second World

Czechoslovakia, East Germany, Poland, the Soviet Union, and other communist or socialist countries in Eastern Europe. You have 9% of the world's population and 18% of the world's wealth. Your share is four treats.

Card #3: Third World

Afghanistan, Algeria, Bangladesh, Bolivia, Brazil, Kampuchea, Chad, China, Egypt, Ethiopia, Ghana, Haiti, India, Indonesia, Iran, Mali, Mexico, Nicaragua, Pakistan, Peru, Vietnam, Zaire, and many other countries. You have 74% of the world's population and 26% of the world's wealth. Your share is five treats.

Table Set-Up

Divide the treats as described on the menu cards. Place each group of treats on a separate plate, and set them on a table. Put the appropriate menu card next to its plate, and cover all the plates with cloth.

Put all the tokens into a bag from which they can be drawn without being seen.

Procedure

Invite participants to take part in a simulation about the distribution of the world's food and other resources. Explain that they will represent groups of countries and that their snack will depend on how wealthy their countries are.

Ask each participant to draw a token from the bag and gather with others who have drawn a similar token. (Note that a Second World person may have no one with whom to gather.) Remove the cloth from the table, and ask the young people to go to the menu card that corresponds to their token.

When all have gathered next to their menu card, have one person in each group read the menu card aloud.

Session 6 ◆ What About War and Peace?

Goals for Participants

- to explore their own feelings and thoughts about conflict, war, and peace in both interpersonal and international relations
- to understand better their own values about conflict, violence, and peace.

Overview

In this session participants explore their own beliefs and feelings about the role of conflict and violence in human affairs, on both interpersonal and international levels. It helps them understand their own tendencies to fight and to manage or avoid conflict.

You may be tempted to judge the young people's more militaristic and fight-oriented expressions and to praise their more peace-oriented responses. In this session, it is important to avoid both of these reactions because the goal is to facilitate an open and honest expression of the young people's beliefs and feelings. Help participants develop a deeper sensitivity to the issues of conflict, war, and peace without advocating your own set of values.

Be aware that there are many questions raised for exploration in this session. Facilitate a breadth of coverage rather than delving into one issue in great depth. Encourage wide participation by the young people as you keep the group moving through this session's activities.

A list of relevant terms and definitions appears in Handout 5. Introduce these terms to clarify particular values that might be expressed. For example, if someone explains that he or she would not fight under any circumstance, you can note that this position is called pacifism.

Materials

- Newsprint, markers, and tape
- Copies of Handout 3, "Refléction Questions—A," for half of the group, and copies of Handout 4, "Reflection Questions—B," for the other half
- Copies of Handout 5, "Definitions," for all participants
- A copy of the role-plays to be used
- A chalice, candle, and matches

Preparation

- Prepare two newsprint charts, one entitled "Personal Conflict Situations" and the other entitled "National Conflict Situations" (listed in the back of this session).

- Set up your usual circle.

- Have wall space available to post the Personal Conflict Situations and the National Conflict Situations charts.

- Read the Role-Plays at the end of this session, and decide which ones to use. You may want to write some of your own role-plays for this activity. Make a copy of each role-play that you plan to use.

Session Plan

Gathering   10-15 minutes

Greet participants as they arrive. When the group has gathered, ask them to join you in a circle.

Invite the young people to share briefly something they experienced during the past week that surprised them. When all have shared who wish to, engage everybody in an active game.

Focusing   5-10 minutes

Briefly review the previous sessions, and give an overview of this session. Then say something like: "Do you remember a time when you felt at peace with a group of people? What was happening then? What were your feelings and thoughts?"

Invite responses. Draw out short responses from as many participants as possible.

When all have shared who wish to, ask: "Do you remember a time when you got into a serious fight or argument, or almost did? What was it about? What were your feelings and thoughts? Why did you fight or not fight?"

Invite responses as before.

Reflecting   5-10 minutes

Post the Personal Conflict Situations chart. Ask for yes or no responses to each question through a show of hands. (Participants should indicate their first reactions.) Record the number of affirmative responses next to each question.

When you have asked all of the questions, note the ones that drew the most affirmative responses. Ask people to comment on why they think these particular situations would be most likely to provoke violence.

When you have concluded this discussion, post the National Conflict Situations. Follow the same procedure with this chart.

Exploring   15-20 minutes

Divide the group into two small groups. Separate the small groups as much as possible.

Give one group copies of Handout 3, and the other group copies of Handout 4. Ask people to consider the questions for a minute and then discuss their responses.

After eight to 10 minutes, gather the whole group. Distribute copies of Handout 5, and discuss the terms. Have one small group share its reflection questions and some of its responses, then have the second small group do the same.

Encourage general discussion of these issues for a few minutes.

Integrating   15-20 minutes

Explain that you'd like the group to act out a few role-plays related to conflict, violence, and peace. Explain that a role-play involves acting out a situation as if it were real. Elicit volunteers for the first role-play. Hand the role-play to the volunteers, and give them a minute to read it and prepare. Then have them begin.

After a few minutes, or when the role-play loses direction or energy, call a halt. Engage the group in discussing the role-play. Invite the role-players to share their experience of acting out this scene.

Continue this procedure with additional role-plays as time allows.

Closing   3-5 minutes

Gather the group in a circle. Give a brief preview of the next session. Then place the chalice in the center of the circle, and have a participant light it. Say:

"As Unitarian Universalists we seek the goal of peace in our world community. May this flame inspire us to work through conflict toward understanding."

Allow a few moments of silence. If desired, engage the young people in singing a song. Then have a participant extinguish the chalice. Say goodbye.

Reflection and Planning

Consider these questions, and discuss them with your co-leader(s):

1. What went well today?

2. What could have been improved? How?

3. What were the patterns of response to the hypothetical conflict situations?

4. What preparation do I need to do for the next session?

Personal Conflict Situations

Would you be willing to fight if...

1. Someone your age whom you could identify stole your younger brother's or sister's bicycle?

2. Someone whom you could identify stole your wallet?

3. You saw someone your age mistreating a helpless younger child?

4. You saw someone your age mistreating your younger sister or brother?

5. Someone strongly insulted your father or mother in public?

6. Someone strongly insulted you in public?

7. Someone your age were about to hit your friend for no apparent reason?

8. Someone your age were about to hit you for no apparent reason?

National Conflict Situations

Should our country go to war if...

1. One of our country's passenger ships is sunk by another country's navy?

2. Our main oil supply is cut off by another country's military?

3. A section of our country declares its independence as a separate nation?

4. One of our country's embassies is bombed by its host country's military?

5. An ally of our country is attacked by a third nation?

6. Our President/Prime Minister is killed by another country's military?

7. A nuclear bomb is dropped on a large city in our country by another country's military?

8. Our planet is attacked by extra-terrestrial aliens?

Role-Plays

(Note: Feel free to change the names or sexes of characters in these role-plays.)

- Mary Ann locks her bike at a bike rack and walks away. When she happens to look back from a distance, she sees a person who looks suspicious standing next to the bike and looking at it. Mary Ann runs back to confront the person.

- Ray always sits in the same seat on the school bus. It's the one all the way in the back. One morning he gets on the bus, and discovers that a new kid is sitting in "his" seat.

- At a youth conference, Alice meets someone her own age from the Soviet Union. Irina says that her country is the best country in the world, that people have a better life in the Soviet Union. What does Alice say?

- Hector overhears Larry telling some other kids what Hector feels is a lie about his best friend. What does Hector say?

Unit Three ◆ Peace and Justice–The Unitarian Universalist Story and Vision

This unit introduces participants to a wide variety of Unitarian Universalists who have contributed to peacemaking and justice-building in North America and throughout the world. These Unitarians, Universalists, and Unitarian Universalists range from eighteenth- and nineteenth-century figures like Benjamin Rush, Elizabeth Cady Stanton, and Emily Stowe, to contemporaries like Linus Pauling and social activists from your own congregation.

One purpose of the unit is to help participants understand more fully the historical commitment of Unitarian Universalists to peace and justice in their communities, their nations, and throughout the world. A second purpose is to encourage participants to feel their own connection to this Unitarian Universalist commitment and tradition.

Please examine Session 9 now, as it requires preparation several weeks in advance.

Also note that this unit includes an optional session, *Meeting of the Minds*, which requires four adults to enact the roles of particular Unitarian Universalists. If you can recruit appropriate adults for this performance, you will find the session to be a valuable and entertaining activity. Read the optional session now so you can make a decision and the necessary preparations.

Session 7 ♦ The Unitarian Universalist Story and Vision

Goals for Participants

- to consider the principles of the Unitarian Universalist Association as stated in the 1985 Principles and Purposes
- to be aware of many historically significant Unitarian Universalist social activists
- to understand how the efforts of these social activists relate to Unitarian Universalist principles
- to gain a historical perspective of the Unitarian Universalist story and vision for peace and social justice.

Overview

This session acquaints participants with some major aspects of the Unitarian Universalist story and vision for peace and social justice. The young people consider the principles of the UUA and learn about many significant actions and events in our denominational past and present that are part of the Unitarian Universalist commitment to peace and social justice.

Please note that this session includes an alternate plan, focusing on the UU Peace and Social Justice Game. Consider both the session plan and the alternate plan and decide which activities to use with your group. Or you may wish to use the game as the central activity in an additional session.

Materials

- Newsprint, markers, and masking tape
- A 6' to 8' length of butcher paper or similar sturdy paper
- Copies of Handout 6, "Unitarian Universal Principles"
- One copy of the People and Event Cards, provided at the back of this session
- Chalice, candle, and matches

Preparation

- Set up your usual circle.
- Have work tables and chairs available for banner-making.
- Make a copy of the People and Event Cards, mount them on cardboard, and cut them out.
- Prepare the butcher paper for the timeline activity by printing the following heading in large letters across the top: Peace and Social Justice: The Unitarian Universalist Story and Vision. Draw a straight line from the left side of the paper to the right, about a third of the distance up from the bottom of the paper. Measure intervals on the line for each 25-year period from 1700 to the present. Mark these intervals with vertical lines. Write the dates from 1700 to the present below the horizontal line. Then post the timeline on the wall.
- If possible, collect library books with pictures of the historical people in this session. Bookmark the pictures so you can find them quickly.

Session Plan

Gathering   8-12 minutes

Greet participants as they arrive. When the group has gathered, ask people to join you in the circle. Invite participants to share briefly something that happened to them in the previous week that was funny. Then engage the young people in an active game.

Focusing   12-14 minutes

In a few sentences, review what the group has experienced in this program. Note that this session begins a new unit. Briefly describe the focus of this unit, and give a quick overview of this session.

Distribute copies of Handout 6 and ask the young people to read it. When they have done so, explain that these statements are not the actual language of the UUA Principles, but they do express the main ideas. Note that this statement of principles was created through a process that included thousands of Unitarian Universalists in every province and state in the years 1983-85.

Invite questions and comments about the principles, and respond as is useful.

Invite the group to create banners that illustrate the principles. Suggest that they choose the principle that most interests them or that they find most important. Have participants make their choices and gather in groups based on those choices.

Allow people to work alone, in pairs, or in trios. If a principle has attracted more than three people, encourage one or more to choose another principle.

Have the markers and newsprint available at the work tables. Tell people they have about eight minutes to work on their banners, and ask them to begin.

You may want to play a song tape of peace and justice music while they work. If a banner is not being made for any of the principles, make a banner by printing the principle(s) on a sheet of newsprint.

Reflecting   5-9 minutes

When participants have completed their banners, gather the group in a circle and have them post the banners around the room in the following way:

Ask one person or group to go first. Have that person or group tape the banner to the wall and respond to the question "What does this principle mean to you?" Then have the person or group describe one experience that relates to this principle.

Follow the same procedure with the other persons or groups. If you have created any banners yourself, post them in the same way.

Exploring   18-25 minutes

Gather the group before the timeline. Tell them that you'd like to introduce an activity that helps them learn about Unitarian Universalists who have worked to support the principles they have just posted around the room.

Divide the People and Events Cards as evenly as possible among the young people. Explain that each card lists a Unitarian Universalist person or event from the past or present, and that the person or event relates to one or more of the UUA Principles. Note that the task is for people to place these cards appropriately on the timeline.

Ask a volunteer to read aloud one of her or his cards. Elicit questions from the volunteer and the group about what the card says, and respond to those questions. Show any pictures that you have of this person or event.

Be sure that people understand the specific terms on the card and its overall meaning. Be aware that you will probably need to explain some of the historical context surrounding this person or event and to define some of the terms.

When the participants understand the card, have the volunteer tape it to the timeline in its appropriate location.

Follow this procedure with the rest of the cards, clarifying each card as needed and encouraging appropriate discussion. Keep the activity moving along.

Integrating and Closing   5-8 minutes

Gather the group in a circle. Invite each participant to respond to the following questions:

• Which person you have learned about today interests you the most?

• What is interesting to you about this person?

When all have shared who wish to, give the group a brief preview of the next session. Then have a participant light the candle. Say, "As Unitarian Universalists, we affirm the living tradition that grows from our proud past. May this flame be a symbol of the wisdom that we can inherit from those who have gone before us."

Allow a few moments of silence. If desired, engage the group in singing a song. Then have a participant extinguish the chalice. Say goodbye.

Reflection and Planning

Consider these questions, and discuss them with your co-leader(s):

1. How do I feel about this session?

2. What was the best part of this session? Why?

3. What did I like least about this session? Why?

4. What preparation do I need to do for the next session?

An Alternate Plan: The UU Peace and Justice Game

The UU Peace and Justice Game requires most of an hour. If you choose to use this in the session, incorporate it by adjusting the session as follows:

Gathering: as it appears in the session plan

Focusing: as in the session plan prior to making banners

Reflecting,
Exploring,
Integrating: playing the game

Closing: as it appears in the session plan.

Object of the Game

The object of the game is to gain the most points in the time allotted for play. (For a longer game, play until all of the game cards have been used and/or no player can successfully play a card.)

Game Cards

There are two kinds of game cards: People and Events Cards (25) and Principles Cards (10: five cards, with two of each card).

Number of Players

Up to six people can play the game at once. More people can play if people play as pairs. If your group is larger than eight or nine, it is recommended that you set up more than one game.

Preparation

1. Photocopy the People and Events Cards, mount them on cardboard, and cut them out.

2. Make two photocopies of the Principles Cards, provided at the back of the session. Mount them on cardboard, and cut them out.

3. Arrange one set of Principles Cards as shown below, so that these cards create the game board.

4. Have a dealer shuffle the rest of the cards, including the other set of Principles Cards, and deal four cards to each player, one at a time, face down.

Playing the Game

1. When the cards are dealt, players pick up their cards and examine them without showing their cards to other players. Players choose which cards they want to play. Play is initiated by the first person to the dealer's left.

2. The game is played by placing a card to the top, bottom, or either side of any card already on the board. A card can be played only if the player can explain a relationship or connection between the card he or she is playing and the card already on the board as described below:

Arrangement of Principles Cards

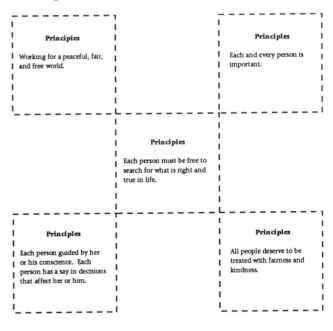

- When placing a People and Events Card next to a Principles Card on the board, the player must explain a relationship between an issue or event listed on the People and Events Card and the principle listed on the Principles Card.

- When placing a Principles Card next to a People and Events Card on the board, the player must explain a relationship between the principle on the card and an issue or event listed on the People and Events Card.

- When placing a People and Events Card next to a card of the same kind, the player must explain a relationship between issues noted on the two cards.

- A Principles Card may not be placed next to another Principles Card.

- A player may place a card next to more than one card on the board. The player can play a card in this situation only if she or he can successfully explain the relationship of the card to all contiguous cards.

3. The other players in the game judge the accuracy and/or validity of the relationship(s) described by the player. If there is disagreement, the leader makes the final decision.

4. The player has one opportunity to play a card during each round.

- If her or his play is accepted, she or he draws another card from the deck (if any cards remain), and it becomes the turn of the next player on the left.

- If her or his play is not accepted, she or he must keep the card that she or he attempted to play, and it becomes the turn of the next player on the left.

- If a player cannot play, she or he must pass.

5. The game is scored as follows:

- Placing a People and Events Card next to either another People and Events Card or a Principles Card earns one point.

- Placing a Principles Card next to a People and Events Card earns two points.

- People earn the allotted number of points for every connection they successfully make in a turn. For example, a People and Events Card successfully placed between two Principles Cards earn two points, one for each relationship.

- Each player keeps track of his or her own score.

6. The game ends when time runs out or when no player can successfully play another card.

Comments

Keep in mind that the primary purpose of the game is learning. Interact with the participants during the game in ways that promote this goal. Be prepared to resolve disputes that may arise.

People and Events

Beacon Press publishes "The Pentagon Papers" in 1971. The press, owned by the UUA, published these secret documents to expose U.S. government lies about the Vietnam War.

People and Events

Julia Ward Howe (1819-1910) Suffragist, peace activist, Unitarian. Writer of "The Battle Hymn of the Republic," Howe later championed the cause of peace, establishing Mother's Peace Day — the original Mother's Day — in 1873.

People and Events

Mary A. Livermore (1820-1905) Abolitionist, suffragist, Universalist. Livermore distributed food, clothing, and medicine to soldiers during the U.S. Civil War. Later she worked for women's right to vote.

People and Events

Massachusetts Peace Society founded by Unitarians in 1815. It was one of the first societies of this kind in the world.

People and Events

Horace Mann (1796-1859) Educator, Unitarian. Mann worked to create public schools for all children. He also fought for humane treatment of the insane and for the abolition of slavery. "Be ashamed to die until you have won some victory for humanity," he wrote.

People and Events

Susan B. Anthony (1820-1906) Suffragist, pacifist, Unitarian. A champion of women's rights, Anthony was arrested and tried for voting in the U. S. election of 1872, when women were still denied the right to vote.

People and Events

Elizabeth Cady Stanton
(1815-1902) Suffragist, Unitarian.
She organized the Seneca Falls,
N.Y., Convention, the first
meeting in the U.S. to consider
"the social, civil, and religious
condition and rights of women."
She was the leading writer of the
women's movement in the 19th
century.

People and Events

John Haynes Holmes (1879-
1964) Social activist, Unitarian
minister. A pacifist during World
War I, he was active in many
liberal causes, including the
NAACP and the ACLU. He
founded the Unitarian Fellowship
for Social Justice.

People and Events

Benjamin Rush (1745-1813)
Physician, revolutionary,
Universalist. Rush condemned
capital punishment, called for the
abolition of slavery, and urged
better treatment for criminals and
the insane. He signed the U.S.
Declaration of Independence.

People and Events

Adin Ballou (1803-1890)
Pacifist, abolitionist, Universalist
minister. He founded the
Hopedale Community in 1842.
Members promised never to hate
or engage in any kind of violence.

People and Events

Lucy Stone (1813-1893) Abolitionist, suffragist, Unitarian.
She was a speaker and activist who
opposed slavery and supported
women's rights. She refused to pay
taxes because she was not allowed
to vote.

People and Events

Theodore Parker (1810-1860)
Scholar, abolitionist, Unitarian
minister. He aided escaped slaves
through the Underground
Railroad and protested the
Fugitive Slave Law. He believed
that the church must care for
people.

People and Events

Clarence Skinner (1881-1949) Pacifist, activist, Universalist minister. As a pacifist, he protested World War I. He founded the Universalist Social Service Commission. He believed that religion should help create a society in which all people could have a good life.

People and Events

The National Woman Suffrage Association, formed by Elizabeth Cady Stanton and Susan B. Anthony. **The American Woman Suffrage Association,** formed by Lucy Stone, Julia Ward Howe and Mary Livermore. Both were organized in 1869 and merged into one organization in 1890.

People and Events

Universalist General Reform Association founded in 1847. The Association was involved with a wide range of issues: peace, human rights, prison reform. The Association sought to change society through education.

People and Events

Linus Pauling (1901-   ) Scientist, peace advocate, Unitarian. He won two Nobel Prizes, one for peace and the other for chemistry. His concern about the effects of nuclear radiation helped lead to the Above-Ground Nuclear Test Ban Treaty between the U.S. and U.S.S.R.

People and Events

A. Powell Davies (1902-1957) Writer, activist, Unitarian minister. A popular and influential minister, he opposed the anti-communist "witch-hunting" of the McCarthy era. He helped to found Americans for Democratic Action.

People and Events

Emily Stowe (1831-1903) Physician, suffragist, Unitarian. Against the opposition of medical schools, she became the first Canadian woman physician. She was a pioneer for women's voting and educational rights in Canada.

People and Events

Dorothea Dix (1802-1887)
Humanitarian, reformer,
Unitarian. She worked for better
conditions for prisoners, the
disabled, and the insane. During
the Civil War, she was the
Superintendent of Nurses for the
Union Army.

People and Events

**The Unitarian Universalist
Service Committee organized
in 1939.** The UUSC was formed
to rescue people in Europe who
were threatened by the Nazis. The
UUSC works to help people in
many parts of the world achieve
independence and self-sufficiency.

People and Events

Clara Barton (1821-1912)
Nurse, humanitarian, Unitarian.
She was a battlefield nurse during
the Civil War. Later she
established the American Red
Cross and became its first
president, directing many of its
relief efforts.

People and Events

**The Unitarian Universalist
Peace Network founded in
1984.** This coalition of Unitarian
Universalist groups works to stop
the nuclear arms race.

People and Events

Whitney Young (1921-1971)
Civil rights leader, Unitarian.
Trained as a social worker, he
became Director of the National
Urban League, an important civil
rights organization. He worked to
improve the life of black people
in the U.S.

People and Events

Albert Schweitzer (1875-1965)
Physician, philosopher, humanitarian, Unitarian. Trained as a
musician and philosopher, he
became a doctor and established a
clinic in Africa. He was inspired
by his "reverence for life."

People and Events

Brock Chisolm (1896-1971) Psychiatrist, humanitarian, Unitarian. Director of Medical Services in the Canadian Army, then Director of the World Health Organization of the United Nations, he was an activist in promoting peace and understanding among peoples and nations.

Principles

Each person must be free to search for what is right and true in life.

Principles

Working for a peaceful, fair, and free world.

Principles

Each and every person is important.

Principles

Each person guided by her or his conscience. Each person has a say in decisions that affect her or him.

Principles

All people deserve to be treated with fairness and kindness.

Session 8 ◆ A Closer Look

Goals for Participants

- to learn about two Unitarian Universalist historical figures, Susan B. Anthony and Henry David Thoreau, and the social issues that concerned them
- to explore their own values and beliefs about these issues and about Anthony's and Thoreau's actions in relation to the issues.

Overview

Events in the lives of Henry David Thoreau and Susan B. Anthony offer illustrations of actions taken in public life that were motivated by principles founded in Unitarian and Universalist traditions. Thoreau's refusal to pay taxes to support a war he could not approve, and Anthony's voting in defiance of the law she considered unjust are both powerful examples of civil disobedience. These actions have provided an inspiration and a model for many others who have accepted risk and sacrifice in the struggle for social justice and peace.

In this session, participants explore these actions by enacting short dramatic presentations. Many young people enjoy this kind of activity, so this session offers both fun and intellectual and emotional engagement.

Note that each play excerpt includes a stop action direction in its script. The discussions that take place at these points encourage the young people to reflect on the issues involved in the actions of Thoreau and Anthony and to examine these figures' choices both from their own points of view and from those of their critics.

Note that while Henry David Thoreau was never formally a Unitarian, he participated in intellectual circles that were primarily composed of Unitarians. He both influenced, and was influenced by, many major Unitarian figures of his time. Some historians dispute his identification as a Unitarian. However, we believe it is appropriate to include his story here, because it gives insight into the wider Unitarian and Universalist ethos of that time.

Please note that the materials listed below include props for both plays. We urge you to gather at least a few props for each play, as even a few key props can help to transform a reading into a genuine piece of drama.

You may want to suggest to your group that they perform one or both of these plays for a group of younger children in your religious education program; for example, children in grades four through six. If the participants are interested in doing this, work out the necessary arrangements.

Materials

- Seven copies of the excerpt from *The Night Thoreau Spent in Jail*, by Jerome Lawrence and Robert E. Lee, and six copies of *Susan B. Anthony*, by Thomas Mikelson (stories appear in this session).
- Props for both plays: a robe and gavel for the judge; scissors and apron for the barber; items of period clothing, and so on
- Chalice, candle, and matches

Preparation

- Set up your usual circle.

- Set up an area for the stage, with chairs available to suggest the various scenes.

- Read the excerpts from the two plays and decide which will be enacted first. Then decide if you will ask for volunteers or if you will assign people to play parts. If the latter, consider who might be appropriate for the various parts.

- Read an encyclopedia article or comparable source about Thoreau and Anthony, and be prepared to give two- to three-minute introductions of each person.

Session Plan

Gathering   5-10 minutes

Greet participants as they arrive. When the group has gathered, ask people to join you in the circle. Invite participants to describe how they are feeling today in one word. Then briefly review what the group has done in previous weeks, and give people an overview of this session.

You may want to omit the active game in this session, so that you have the maximum amount of time available for the plays.

Focusing and Reflecting   5-10 minutes

Explain the rules for the values whip as follows:

You pose a question to the group. Participants have a few moments to consider an answer. Then you "whip" around the group, calling on people to share brief responses. People may choose to pass. Tell them that they will have a few more minutes after the whip to discuss in greater depth any of the issues or concerns that come up.

Make sure everyone understands the rules. Then ask the following questions or ones of your choosing:

- If you could change one thing today in your school, what would you change?

- If you could change one thing today in this world, what would you change?

- If you could change one thing today in this church or fellowship, what would you change?

- What is something you believe in strongly?

When you have completed the whip, invite comments and questions. Encourage appropriate discussion for a few minutes.

Exploring   35-45 minutes

Introduce this activity by saying something like: "Today we have a couple of short plays to perform that will help us to know more about two people who are characteristic of the many Unitarian Universalists who have chosen to act from their principles. These two people are Susan B. Anthony

and Henry David Thoreau. Both chose to act from their principles and helped to further those principles by their example. As we act out these short plays, we'll be looking for the principles that guided them."

Invite participants to explain what a principle is. (A principle is a basic truth that is used as a guide to action.) Ask people to share some examples of principles. Then designate the actors for the first play in the way you have chosen, and hand out the scripts. Involve the actors in setting the stage. Then give a two- to three-minute introduction of the protagonist of the play.

Inform the actors and the audience of the stop action element in the script, so they will be prepared for it. Then ask the actors to begin the play.

When the actors reach the stop action, explore the appropriate set of questions below with the group for a few minutes, giving as many people as possible an opportunity to share.

When the actors have completed the play, gather the group and invite people to raise any other comments or questions for discussion.

Follow the same procedure with the second play.

Stop Action Questions

The Night Thoreau Spent in Jail

- What are the issues involved here?

- How does this look from Henry's perspective? From Sam's?

- What principle is guiding Henry?

- Are there other ways he could have made his point?

- What would you do under these circumstances?

- What do you think will happen?

Susan B. Anthony

- What are the issues involved here?

- What is the situation from Jones's and Smith's perspectives? From Anthony's?

- What principle is guiding Anthony?

- Are there other ways she could do this?

- What would you do under these circumstances?

- What do you think will happen?

Integrating   4-8 minutes

Engage participants in discussing these questions:

- What were Anthony and Thoreau trying to do by their actions?

- Do you think their actions were effective?

Closing   3-5 minutes

Give the group a preview of the next session. Then place the chalice in the center of the group, and have a participant light it. Say, "As Unitarian Universalists, we affirm the heroic deeds of those Unitarian Universalists who came before us. May this flame remind us of those who sought to act according to their principles."

Allow a few moments of silence. If desired, engage the participants in singing a song. Then have a participant extinguish the chalice. Say goodbye.

Reflection and Planning

Consider these questions, and discuss them with your co-leader(s):

1. What was the best part of this session? The worst?

2. If I were to lead this session again, how would I change it?

3. What preparation do I need to do for the next session?

The Night Thoreau Spent in Jail

From the play by Jerome Lawrence
and Robert E. Lee

Narrator: In May of 1846, the United States declared war on Mexico. Many people opposed the war, especially abolitionists in the North who feared that it would result in extending slavery into the Southwest. Henry David Thoreau was one of these people. In disgust and defiance, he refused to pay his poll-tax, amounting to about $1.50. With Thoreau, it was a matter of principle. Nevertheless, a warrant was issued for his arrest. The local constable caught up with him on a day in late July, 1846, when Thoreau left his cabin at Walden Pond to go into Concord to have a shoe repaired.

Sam: Look, it don't pleasure me none, servin' a court order on you. Sometimes this is an unpleasant job!

Henry: Then quit. If you don't like being a constable, Sam, resign.

Sam: Somebody's got to do the work of the people.

Henry: Are you going to arrest me?

Sam: I don't want to, Henry. But the government gets persnickety about taxes when we got a war goin'.

Henry: I will not pay one copper penny to an unjust government!

Sam: If the majority says —

Henry: I'm the majority. A majority of one!

Deacon Ball: *(From the edge of a crowd that has gathered.)* Arrest him!

Henry: Go ahead, Constable. But I'll tell you this, if one thousand... If one hundred... If ten men... ten honest men only... If one honest man in this state of Massachusetts had the conviction and the courage to withdraw from this unholy partnership and let himself be locked up in the County Jail, it'd be the start of more true freedom than we've seen since a few farmers had the guts to block the British up by the road.

Another Voice: Lawbreaker!

Henry: What law ever made men free? Men have got to make the law free. And if a law is wrong, by Heaven, it's the duty of man to stand up and say so. Even if your oddfellow society wants to clap him in jail.

Farmer: That's revolution!

Henry: Yes, sir, that's revolution! What do you think happened at Concord Bridge? A prayer meeting?

Sam: What are you tryin' to do, Henry? Wipe out all the laws?

Henry: As many as possible.

Deacon Ball: Throw him in jail!

Henry: What are you waiting for, Sam? Get out the chains. Drag me off to jail.

Sam: There must be somethin' almighty wrong when a man's so willin' to go!

Henry: Sam, it's very simple. What the government of this country is doing turns my stomach! And if I keep my mouth shut, I'm a criminal. To my conscience. To my God. To my society. And to you, Sam Staples. You want a dollar from me? If I don't approve of the way that dollar's spent, you're not going to get it!

Sam: All I know is, it ain't fittin' to throw a Harvard man in jail. 'Specially a Thoreau. An honester man than you, Henry, I never knew.

Henry: Is that a compliment, Sam?

Sam: Yes, sir.

Henry: Well, thanks. Now clap me in your Bastille. *(Henry holds his hands out in front of him. Sam leads Henry off to jail and puts him in a cell.)*

Stop Action

Sam: It ain't much, but it's clean. *(He takes out a ledger book.)* Now, Henry, I gotta put down your age.

Henry: Twenty-nine summers.

Sam: *(writing it down)* Twenty-nine. Occupation?

Henry: What am I? *(thinking)* Oh, Ho-er of beans. Fisherman. Inspector of snowstorms...

Sam: Them won't do.

Henry: You want respectable trades? Let's see. Pencil-maker; occasionally. Schoolteacher—once. Surveyor. Carpenter. Author—alleged. Huckleberry-hunter—expert.

Sam: *(Writing)* Carpenter. That'll do. *(Pleading)* Please pay up, Henry.

Henry: If you ask me to pay for a rifle, Sam, it's the same as asking me to fire it! You're making me as much a killer as the foot-soldier who crashes across the border into faraway Mexico, charges into his neighbor's house, sets fire to it and kills his children!

Ralph Waldo Emerson: Henry! Henry! What are you doing in jail?

Henry: Waldo! What are you doing out of jail?

Narrator: The next day, Thoreau was released from jail. Someone had paid his fine. (It is said that Thoreau was quite angry that someone had done this.) He wrote an account of his experience, along with a lengthy explanation of his motives, in a famous essay entitled, "Civil Disobedience." The essay was an inspiration for such people as Mahatma Gandhi and Martin Luther King, Jr.

Susan B. Anthony

by Thomas Mikelson

Narrator: In the years after the Civil War, it was still impossible for women in the United States to vote in elections. Here and there across the country, a few women were testing the laws by trying to register to vote. As the elections of 1872 drew near, Susan B. Anthony was at her home in Rochester, New York, resting between speaking tours. She had been following the progress of women in their struggle to vote and she was eager to test this issue herself. The first step would be to register to vote. With that intention, she went to the local barbershop, where the registration headquarters was located.

(Barbershop with Mr. Jones, the barber, shaving a customer in a chair. Mr. Smith, the registrant, is sitting in a chair with the registration book in front of him.)

Jones: Hello, Miss Anthony. I haven't seen you for some time. What brings you here?

Anthony: Good morning, Mr. Jones. I am home in Rochester for a while now visiting my family. I am here to register to vote in the upcoming election.

Jones: Well, Miss Anthony, I guess you will have to talk to Mr. Smith, the voter registrant, about that.

Anthony: Very well. Good morning, Mr. Smith. I have come to register to vote in the coming election.

Smith: I can't do that, Miss Anthony. I haven't ever registered a woman voter. They wouldn't allow it.

Jones: I reckon you're correct there, Mr. Smith. They wouldn't like it one bit.

Anthony: Gentleman, I'll worry about their feelings, if you don't mind. I want to vote. And now I want to register.

Smith: You don't understand, Miss Anthony. I cannot do that. They wouldn't like it. I might lose my job. You have no right to put me in this position.

Anthony: I have no right! Is that what you say? I have no right? But you have a right to keep me from registering to vote. Rights seem to be strange things. Now, if you please, I will register to vote.

Jones: Miss Anthony, you don't understand. Mr. Smith is right. You are not allowed to vote. He cannot register you. We just enforce the laws. Why don't you go home?

Anthony: Gentlemen, I intend to register. I intend to vote. I am fully ready to undergo any consequences of my choice. Now I wish to sign the book.

Jones: Go ahead, Smith. Let her register. I'll vouch for you over at the courthouse. They won't let her vote anyway.

Smith: All right, Miss Anthony. Sign here.

Anthony: Thank you, gentlemen *(signing the book)*. I'll see you at the polls. Don't forget to vote!

Narrator: Miss Anthony did vote on November fifth, along with a small number of other women she had gathered together. Days passed and nothing happened. Then, on the evening of November 18th, a U.S. deputy marshall rang her doorbell. He announced that he had come to arrest her. It was decided that Miss Anthony would be tried in federal court. The trial was held in June, 1873. Her counsel was longtime acquaintance Henry Seldon. The judge was Ward Hunt, who had been recently appointed to the bench.

Seldon: Miss Anthony is not guilty. She is charged only because she is a woman. If the act in question had been done by her brother it would not only have been lawful, it would have been considered honorable. Miss Anthony voted in good faith, believing that the Constitution of the United States guarantees her the right to vote as surely as it guarantees the right of any man. The Fourteenth and Fifteenth Amendments of the Constitution are the basis of her right to vote. Your honor, it would appear that Miss Anthony's only real crime is her attempt to secure her legal rights under the Constitution of the United States.

Stop Action

Narrator: For several hours the arguments went on. Finally, at the end of the arguments, without any hesitation, Judge Hunt drew out an already prepared written document and began to read.

Hunt: "The legislature of the State of New York has seen fit to say that the franchise of voting shall be limited to the male sex. If the Fifteenth Amendment had contained the word 'sex,' the argument of the defendant would have been potent... The Fourteenth Amendment gives no right to a woman to vote, and the voting of Miss Anthony was in violation of the law... Upon the evidence, I suppose there is no question for the jury and that the jury should be directed to find a verdict of guilty."

Seldon: *(Springing to his feet.)* Your Honor, I object! Members of the jury, you do have a question and I urge you to consider the issues carefully and decide whether or not the defendant is guilty of a crime.

Hunt: Objection overruled! The question, gentlemen of the jury, in the form it finally takes, is wholly a question of the law. And I have decided as a question of the law that Miss Anthony is not protected under the Fourteenth Amendment. She did not have the right to vote. I therefore direct you to find her guilty.

Seldon: That is a direction that no court has the power to take in a criminal case.

Hunt: Has the prisoner anything to say why sentence shall not be pronounced?

Anthony: *(Rising)* Yes, Your Honor, I have many things to say, for in your ordered verdict of guilty, you have trampled underfoot every vital principle of our government; my natural rights, my civil rights, my political rights, my judicial rights, are all alike ignored...

Hunt: I protest, Miss... *(Anthony goes on.)*

Anthony: May it please the court, Your Honor, I am not arguing the question but simply stating the reasons why sentence cannot in justice be pronounced against me. Your denial of my citizen's right to vote is the denial of my right of consent as one of the governed, the denial of my right of representation as one of the taxed, the denial of my right to trial by a jury of my peers.

Hunt: The court cannot allow the prisoner to go on... *(Anthony goes on.)*

Anthony: I am not here only for myself, but for all women everywhere.

Hunt: The court must insist...

Anthony: I have been tried by the forms of law all made by men, interpreted by men, administered by men, in favor of men, against women...

Hunt: *(Shouting)* The court orders the prisoner to sit down...

Anthony: Your Honor, I shall never pay a dollar of your unjust penalty. All I posses is a debt of $10,000 incurred by my newspaper, *The Revolution,* which is solely to educate women to do precisely as I have done, rebel against your man-made, unjust, unconstitutional forms of law that tax, fine, imprison, and hang women while they deny them the right of representation in government.

Narrator: The judge finally declared that Miss Anthony not be required to remain in prison pending the payment of her fine. She received no justice in that courtroom, but she made her point before the court and the world. Susan B. Anthony had struck another blow for the freedom of women.

Session 9 ♦ Hearing from Our Own

Goals for Participants

- to learn about ways that members of their own Unitarian Universalist congregation are influenced by their religious beliefs to take actions for peace and justice
- to explore their reactions to the influence of religious beliefs on taking action for peace and justice.

Overview

This session focuses on several members of your congregation, who will share with the participants their motivations and experiences in acting for peace and justice. The last part of the session gives the young people an opportunity to respond to what they have heard by asking questions and offering comments.

Recruit your guest presenters a few weeks prior to the session. Guidelines for recruitment and preparation of the guests are in the Preparation.

Materials

- Nametags for guests, participants, and leaders, if appropriate
- Paper and pens or pencils
- Chalice, candle, and matches
- Photocopies of Questions for Guests (see Preparation)

Preparation

- Place a comfortable chair for each guest at the front of your space. Arrange the chairs for the participants and leader(s) in a semicircle facing the guest chairs. A few weeks prior to this session, recruit four members of your congregation as guests. As much as possible, recruit guests who fit the following criteria:

— they are currently or have been recently involved in activities of peacemaking and/or justice-building

— to a large extent, they are moved to act by their religious values and principles

— they can articulate why and how their religious values and principles motivate them to act as they do in these areas

— they are willing to meet with your group and talk openly about these topics, and they interact comfortably with early adolescents.

- Allow yourself adequate time to find the most appropriate people for this activity. Look for people who are involved in local, district, or denominational social service, social witness, social education, or social action projects. Ask your minister, board president, social responsibility chair, and/or church secretary for suggestions. You may also find people who are active not through your society but through their professions or through volunteer political or service activities. Appropriate guests may not be well known, but may be "quiet heroes." Avoid people considered to be abrasive.

- Try to organize a balanced panel, with both women and men, people of different ages and backgrounds, people active in both peace and justice causes, and so on. However, as your range of choices is finite, simply do the best you can in striving for balance. The most important qualification may be the capacity to communicate with early adolescents in an open and honest way.

- When you have recruited your guests, give them a copy of the Questions for Guests, which appear in this session. Ask them to be prepared to talk about themselves in relation to these questions for about five to seven minutes. Let each guest know who the other guests will be. Finally, ask the guests to arrive 10 minutes before the session begins.

- When your guests arrive, explain the plan for the session. Invite them to take part in all of the group's activities. Remind them how long you want them to speak in their presentations.

Session Plan

Gathering   8-10 minutes

Greet participants as they arrive. If you are using nametags, hand them out as people enter the room. If you ask the participants to wear nametags, be sure that you and the guests also wear them.

When the group has gathered, ask people to take a seat in the semicircle. Direct the guests to their seats.

Introduce the guests to the participants, or have them introduce themselves. Ask the young people to introduce themselves to your guests.

Give the group a brief overview of this session. Then engage everyone in playing an active game.

Focusing   2 minutes

Gather the group in the semicircle and chairs, and say something like: "In the last few sessions we have learned about Unitarian Universalists who have worked for peace and justice in the past. But our caring about and commitment to peace and justice didn't end then. It goes on now. Our guests today are Unitarian Universalists from our own congregation who are working for peace and justice now. And each of them will tell you something about this."

Exploring   30-40 minutes

Explain that each guest will speak in turn. When all have spoken, there will be time for questions and comments. Hand out paper and pens or pencils, and invite the young people to jot down questions and comments they want to raise.

Invite one of the guests to begin. Be aware of the time, and if necessary, politely remind the guest of the time limit. Follow the same procedure with each guest.

As the guests speak, jot down ideas or questions you want to raise later.

After the second guest has shared, invite everyone to take a quick stretch break. If the young people seem restless at this time, engage them in a quick reprise of the active game they played earlier.

Reflecting and Integrating   12-20 minutes

Invite the young people to raise questions and comments. Let them initiate as much of this discussion as they wish. Allow guests to respond to each other as it serves the interests of the young people, but be sure that the young people's initiative is not overwhelmed by guest interaction. If participants run out of questions and comments, facilitate a continued discussion by directing appropriate questions to the young people and/or guests.

With a few minutes remaining for this activity, ask participants to respond to the question below with a couple of words or a phrase. (This can also be structured as a whip.)

- When you think about what you've heard today, what feels the most helpful (or important, or an adjective of your choice) to you?

Closing   3-5 minutes

Thank the guests for their participation. Then give the group a preview of the next session.

Place the chalice in the center of the semicircle, and have a participant light it. Then say, "As Unitarian Universalists we believe in accepting our responsibility to work for peace and justice in the world. May this flame help us to see more clearly how we as individuals can contribute to the cause of peace and justice."

Allow a few moments of silence. If desired, engage the group in singing a song. Then have a participant extinguish the chalice. Say goodbye to the participants and guests.

Reflection and Planning

Consider these questions, and discuss them with your co-leader(s):

1. What did I like best about this session? Least?

2. What can I learn from my experience of this session?

3. Did anything particularly grab the participants' interest? If so, is there a way to encourage this?

4. What preparation do I need to do for the next session?

Questions for Guests

1. What are your core religious values and principles?

2. In what ways do these religious values and principles influence the way you act in terms of peace and social justice?

3. What struggles have you gone through in acting as you have for peace and justice?

4. What keeps you going with this activity?

5. What can one person really do?

6. Do you have advice about these concerns to share with people of junior high age?

Optional Session ♦ A Meeting of the Minds

Goals for Participants

- to learn about the lives of four Unitarians and Universalists who made a significant contribution to peace and social justice in their times
- to be introduced to several of the great social issues of the nineteenth and early twentieth centuries
- to deepen their sensitivity to peace and justice issues
- to gain a stronger sense of pride in our Unitarian Universalist story and vision.

Overview

The format of this session is based on an old television program called The Meeting of the Minds. The show was hosted by Steve Allen, and it featured actors and actresses portraying well-known historical figures who engaged in fictional discussions of contemporary issues. For example, Aristotle, Machiavelli, and Emma Goldman might discuss the ethics of multinational corporations. Darwin, Schweitzer, and a modern biochemist might explore the ethics of genetic engineering. This format resulted in both fascinating and educational programs.

This session asks you to organize a similar panel discussion about peace and social justice issues. You play the moderator, and you recruit four volunteers — adults and/or high school-age people — to play the following historical figures:

- Adin Ballou (1803-1890): founder of a pacifist commune

- Julia Ward Howe (1819-1910): patriot, feminist, and peacemaker

- Mary Livermore (1820-1905): public servant and reformer

- William Howard Taft (1857-1930): President of the United States, and advocate of peace through international law.

These four figures represent an intriguing variety in terms of gender, denominational background, and outlook on the tasks of peacemaking and justice-building. There are two women and two men; two Unitarians and two Universalists; a pacifist, a "just war" theorist, and one who gave humanitarian aid to both sides in the American Civil War.

Please note that preparation for this session needs to be done over a period of several weeks.

This session is similar in structure to Session 9. If you enact this session as part of your program, do not do it the week after Session 9. Instead, take a week off from this program, and have a party, plan an event, go on a field trip, or whatever. Or enact this session later in the program.

Materials

- Four copies of the Panel Questions, included in this session
- Four copies of each of the Self-Portraits, also in this session
- Notecards and pens or pencils
- A pitcher of water, with four glasses, for the panel
- Cardboard
- Costumes and props for the panelists

Preparation

- Make namecards that will stand on a table in front of each panelist. Have each card include name, dates of birth and death, and a descriptive phrase.

- Set up a table and chairs for the panelists in the front of your space. Set up audience chairs for the participants.

- Place the water glasses and pitcher on the table.

- Place notecards and pencils on the table for each panelist.

- Familiarize yourself with the four Self-Portraits. Consider who in your congregation could play each part well. Dramatic ability is an important factor. Be open to recruiting both adults and people of high school age.

- Recruit four people to play the roles. Give each panelist copies of all four Self-Portraits and a copy of the Panel Questions. Ask people to study their own characters with particular care and to consider how their characters would respond to the various questions. Be sure they know the date and time of their performance.

- If possible, hold a rehearsal prior to the session to clarify expectations, explore the material, and give the panelists practice in answering questions. Emphasize the need for brief, clear responses.

- Arrange for costumes and props that suggest the times in which the characters lived.

- Be prepared to introduce each panelist. Study the Panel Questions so you can use them flexibly as you facilitate the discussion.

- If desired, arrange for someone to audiotape or videotape the panel discussion.

Session Plan

The standard session structure is not used for this session, as the panel creates its own structure.

1. Greet participants as they arrive. When the group has gathered, invite the panelists and the audience to take their seats. Hand out notecards and pencils or pens to participants. Suggest that

they use them to write down questions. Then say something like this to start the panel:

"Welcome to this *Meeting of the Minds*. We're delighted that all of you can be with us today. This is a once-in-a-lifetime occasion, an opportunity to talk with our Universalist and Unitarian foremothers and forefathers. We're eager to hear their thoughts about peace and justice. I have some questions for our distinguished panel, and later the group will be invited to ask questions and share comments."

2. Give a one-minute introduction of each panelist.

3. Engage the panelists in discussion, starting with the first four Panel Questions. Use these questions as a rough guide, but do not be confined by them. Encourage balanced time-sharing by the panelists.

4. Use the other Panel Questions as useful. Introduce current events where appropriate.

5. With about 15 or 20 minutes remaining in the session, actively encourage questions and comments from the audience.

6. At the end of the session, thank everyone for participating, particularly the panelists.

If desired, gather the participants and panelists in a circle. Place the chalice in the center of the circle, and have a participant light it. Say, "As Unitarian Universalists we believe that each person must search for truth and meaning where she or he finds it. May the light of this flame remind us of the importance of our own search."

Allow a few moments of silence. If desired, lead the group in a song. Have a participant extinguish the flame. Then say goodbye to the participants and panelists.

Reflection and Planning

Consider these questions, and discuss them with your co-leader(s):

1. How do I feel about this session?

2. What have I learned from the experience of this session?

3. What preparation do I need to do for the next session?

Panel Questions

1. What are you most proud of as you look back over your life?

2. How important was your Universalism or Unitarianism to the way you lived your life?

3. How can people create a more just society?

4. What is the best course we can take toward world peace?

5. What are your ideas about today's conflict between the United States, Canada, and their allies and the Soviet Union and its allies?

6. What are your views on the current roles of women and men in society?

7. What are your thoughts about relations between people of different races in the world today?

8. What advice to you have for today's young Unitarian Universalists?

Self Portraits

Self-Portrait One:
Adin Ballou (1803-1890)
Founder of a Pacifist Commune

It was my privilege to play an important part in our Unitarian Universalist story and vision. I am most remembered as the founder of the Hopedale Community in Massachusetts, an experiment in putting ideals into practice. My vision was of people actually living, day by day, according to the principles of fairness, kindness, and peace.

Love must overcome hate in our world. I always felt that studying and talking about religious ideals are only good as a start. We must go further and learn to live according to the highest ideals we know.

My family and relatives, the Ballous, helped to settle the state of Rhode Island, going back in history for several generations. There were almost two dozen Universalist ministers with the last name of Ballou.

My father was very strict, believing in hard work as the most important thing in life. I did my share of the work, but also enjoyed reading. As a youth, I started to look forward to going to college.

When I was 12 years old, something happened that changed my life. A great storm destroyed our hometown: the houses, the orchards, everything. My parents, my brothers, and I believed that God was punishing us for ignoring Him. Suddenly we became truly religious and organized a church. To my disappointment, the excitement about church life died down fairly quickly in my family and the surrounding towns. But my own interest in living the Christian life increased.

At the age of 19, I heard the call of God to preach His Word. I became the minister of the church that had formed after the great storm. Several of my relatives had become Universalist ministers, because Universalists believed that everyone would be saved. I considered this belief dangerous, because it would make people morally lazy, the way we were before the storm.

I decided to study the Bible more closely, along with the Universalist teachings, so I could show my relatives how wrong they were. But the more I learned about the Universalist faith, the more true its message felt to me. I then converted to Universalism myself. This change was a great disappointment to many of my family and friends. I lost their love and felt very much alone in the world. My father even started a campaign to remove me from our church. He succeeded, and I was excommunicated.

I was then free to marry a girlfriend, Abigail, with whom I used to argue about religion. She was a Universalist, and her family now took me in with open arms. We moved to Massachusetts, where I was called by a Universalist church to be its minister.

Among the Universalists, an argument was brewing. Does God save us without question, or does God save us after a period of moral instruction? My view was that we needed to be "restored" to God's favor through a process of divine guidance after death. My church dismissed me, so I withdrew from the Universalists and joined the Restorationists.

For the next 10 years I served a Congregational church. I was free to turn my attention away from theological questions and concentrate on social issues. Despite criticism, I favored temperance, the outlawing of the drinking of alcohol, because I believed that alcoholic beverages weakened moral discipline. I also favored the abolition of slavery and giving women the right to vote.

Gradually I began to feel the need for a different approach to the religious life. Beyond our beliefs about righteousness, we must actually live the Christian faith on a daily basis. It was then that I founded the Hopedale Community as an experiment in practical Christianity, an attempt to really live the law of love.

When I was 39, Hopedale, the major project of my life, began. Twenty-eight of us acquired 250 acres on which to implement our ideals. In the Hopedale Community, we would pursue the pure and simple religion of Jesus. We would never show hatred toward another human being. We would not take oaths, hold public office, or show any loyalty to a power other than God. We would never lift an angry hand against our neighbors, however angry they might become. We would reject all forms of violence, especially war and its preparations. We would share all property and profits equally.

Our beginning years were promising. We cleared the land, restored buildings, planted crops, and raised livestock. We built a school, a printing shop, a sawmill, and a factory. We made hats, shoes, furniture, and sheet iron. And most importantly, we were able to live together lovingly and peacefully for the most part.

During the Civil War, our commune remained pacifist. We knew all too well that war alone could not make the black people free. Their true liberation would require a moral and spiritual conversion on the part of the people of the United States as a whole.

In our communal experiment, certain problems arose and persisted. Despite the patience and goodwill of many of us, enthusiasm faded, tasks were left undone, conflicts emerged, and in some areas profits dwindled.

To my great disappointment, Hopedale dissolved in 1868, after our two largest shareholders withdrew their funds. Most essentially, it was a moral defeat rather than a financial failure, because our early years showed that strong-willed people who know themselves to be God's children can live together lovingly and equitably.

A church survived from this noble experiment, and I served as its minister for 13 years. I lived with some grief, however, over the sudden dimming of our vision. But I took some consolation from my writings and the influence they seemed to have on greater souls. I exchanged letters with Leo Tolstoy, the famous Russian novelist and philosopher. He was among the few who appreciated the ideals for which I lived.

Perhaps someday my vision will take shape again, among the purer of heart and stronger of will.

Self-Portrait Two:
Julia Ward Howe (1819-1910)
Patriot, Feminist, and Peacemaker

It was my privilege to play an important role in our Unitarian Universalist story and vision. I am most remembered as the writer of the words to "The Battle Hymn of the Republic." However, I would rather be remembered as an inspiring advocate of women's development and a prophet of world peace.

My mother died when I was only five years old. Through most of my childhood, I was parented by my strict but well-meaning father. In response to him I developed a capacity for hard work and learning. I was tutored in the classics, languages, literature, philosophy, and music.

At the age of 23, I married a brilliant doctor and medical innovator, Samuel Gridley Howe. He was an energetic Unitarian, whose strong conscience led him to serve the causes of education for the blind, improved conditions for the insane, and reform in public schools.

Though we agreed on many social questions, we were at complete odds about the proper place of women in society. He wanted women to be submissive to men in many ways, and he forbade me to speak in public and publish my poetry. I was unwilling to live with these restrictions, and our marriage was often stormy.

Before the Civil War, we worked together on a magazine serving the cause of the abolition of slavery. We saw the war as a crusade to save our country from the sin of slavery. During the war, we worked with Mary Livermore and others on the Sanitary Commission, bringing hospitals and nurses to the battlefield.

Near the beginning of the war, my Unitarian minister, James Freeman Clarke, suggested that I write some good words for that stirring tune, "John Brown's Body." The result was "The Battle Hymn." After its publication in the *Atlantic Monthly*, it seemed to become the theme song of the Union. Even President Lincoln gave it his blessing.

My two favorite Unitarian ministers, the Rev. Clarke and the Rev. Theodore Parker, both encouraged me to preach in the pulpit. I finally did in 1864 and frequently after that. I am not sure what brought me the deepest satisfaction: speaking, writing, or organizing for worthy causes.

After the war I joined the movement for women's rights, an effort that continued for the rest of my life. Since many good-hearted women worked hard to give the black people their freedom, it seemed only fair that women should now achieve full political equality with men.

I helped to found, and then lead, several important women's organizations. Perhaps my favorite was the New England Women's Club, which encouraged new ideas and higher public roles for women. The elevation of the female half of the human race is the key to progress for all, I believed.

After the outbreak of the Franco-Prussian War in 1870, my social outlook was broadened to include the cause of world peace. It seemed to me that women, and especially mothers, were in an excellent position to avoid all the standard excuses for war and, thereby, to promote peace throughout society and among nations.

I served as president of the Women's International Peace Association. This campaign required much letter-writing and speech-making, the convening of many meetings, and numerous travels. I issued an appeal to womanhood throughout the world. I also attempted to create a new holiday, Mothers' Peace Day, celebrating the natural leadership of women in giving birth to a world free of war.

Looking back at my life, one theme stands out clearly. If we believe in the goodness of people, we can win their cooperation in the making of a better world. Progress is inevitable!

Self-Portrait Three:
Mary Livermore (1820-1905)
Public Servant and Reformer

It was my privilege to play an important role in the Unitarian Universalist story and vision. I am most widely known as a lecturer and reformer in the area of women's rights. During the Civil War, as I helped people on both sides of the battle lines, I became very aware that the emancipation of women could do a great deal toward curing the ills of society. I like to believe that my work, and my long and happy partnership with my husband, Daniel, serve as constructive models both for women and married couples.

My childhood was darkened with fears of damnation. I grew up under strict religious discipline. I had to give an account to my father of how I spent every hour of every day!

A turning point in my religious outlook occurred when my younger sister, a sweet and lovely invalid, died suddenly. My parents believed that since she had not yet been saved, she would have to suffer eternal torment. I rebelled, feeling that I would rather go to hell with my good sister than to heaven with a God who could damn such an innocent soul.

I turned to my studies for relief from my religious worries, did well in school, and graduated with honors from a female academy at the age of 16. After teaching for a year, a wonderful opportunity came my way. I was offered a job as tutor for the children of a wealthy plantation family in Virginia. My father thought my place was at home in Massachusetts and forbade me to go. In fear and trembling, I made my way south to a new life.

As a tutor in Virginia, I saw slavery at first hand, and I became a firm abolitionist thereafter. I also enjoyed the well-stocked library in my plantation home but could not reconcile the liberal views of Thomas Paine and Ethan Allen with the religion of my childhood. There seemed to be more questions than answers in the world of religion.

After three years of tutoring, I returned to Massachusetts and got the job of headmistress at the Duxbury School. I was 22 years old. My parents considered me successful, though not entirely proper as a woman.

Another major change in my religious outlook occurred when I attended a Universalist church one Christmas Eve. I had been taught that Universalists were completely without morals, believing that even sinners would be saved. But I was pleasantly surprised both by the sermon and the young minister, Daniel Livermore. He said that since we are expected to be forgiving, God must be forgiving as well. Otherwise, we are expected to do better than God! I had found my church.

After a year of study and courting with the Rev. Livermore, we were married. He freed me to develop my own religious and political ideas. Though I now lost the family of my upbringing, I had found my soulmate and my calling as a reformer.

I worked as a homemaker and writer during Daniel's 12 years as minister. We worked for abolition, temperance, and women's suffrage, all causes that made us unpopular with our congregations. We decided to leave the parish ministry and take up the ownership and editing of a Universalist newspaper in Chicago. Through this paper, we championed social reform for another 11 years.

During the Civil War, I was chosen to work for the Sanitary Commission by the famous Unitarian minister, Dr. Henry Bellows. We raised almost a million dollars for food, clothing, and medical supplies. I insisted that aid be sent to both sides in the tragic struggle. I talked with President Lincoln several times. He gave me the manuscript of his famous Emancipation Proclamation. We sold his document at auction for $3,000, with the money going to the Sanitary Commission.

After the war, I convened the first women's suffrage convention in the state of Illinois. Soon after this I established a suffrage magazine, *The Agitator*, which was later merged with the *Woman's Journal*.

Beginning in 1870, I spent a quarter-century on the lecture circuit, averaging 150 lectures a year and speaking primarily for the causes of women's rights, political education, and temperance. During this productive but sometimes exhausting period, I served as president of various women's organizations, including the Massachusetts Women's Christian Temperance Union.

Many people considered me an effective public speaker. In any case, speaking was my primary tool as a reformer.

The fiftieth anniversary of my wedding with Daniel was one of the happiest occasions of my life, allowing us to look back over our many journeys and efforts with deep satisfaction. The thought that I helped bring closer the day of several major reforms gave me delight and a sense of fulfillment.

Self-Portrait Four:
William Howard Taft (1857-1930)
President of the United States and Advocate of Peace Through International Law

It was my privilege to play an important role in our Unitarian Universalist story and vision. I am remembered mostly as the twenty-seventh president of the United States and the tenth Chief Justice of the Supreme Court. I was a lifelong Unitarian and had a strong influence on the development of liberal religious social philosophy, especially on issues related to peace.

My view was that peace should be the goal of every nation, though war may be necessary as a step to achieve justice. And justice, in turn, enables us to build the foundations for a lasting peace.

My father was an adviser to President Grant, so I grew up with a deep respect for government and the importance of public service. After college, I served as president of my Unitarian church's young people's group, and it was there that my interest in becoming President began.

At the age of 23, I entered the legal profession and soon became a judge, advancing through both state and federal levels. I became interested in international law. After the Spanish-American War in 1898, I served as president of the Philippine Commission. The United States had taken control of the Philippine Islands during that war, and my job was to organize a colonial government for the islands.

Like my father, I became an adviser to a President. I served as the Secretary of War in President Theodore Roosevelt's cabinet. Then I served as Vice President. In 1908 I ran for President and won.

In my presidency I continued the policies of Mr. Roosevelt. I was a strong believer in national security as well as in strict honesty in government. I established the federal postal-savings system, emphasized the conservation of natural resources, and strictly enforced anti-trust laws.

After my presidency, I taught law at Yale University, promoted the League to Enforce Peace, and later supported the League of Nations. It seemed to me that our best chance of achieving enduring peace was through an effective system of international law.

I also became very active in the Unitarian denomination. I served as vice-president of the American Unitarian Association for six years and as president of the Unitarian General Conference for 10 years. I considered us a small but influential church, due to the high level of education of our members.

A major debate about war and peace broke out among my fellow Unitarians in 1917, just before the United States entered World War I. I was the main spokesperson for the side favoring entry into the war. John Haynes Holmes, a famous minister from New York City, was the main spokesperson for those who opposed all war as a matter of principle.

I believed that Germany had become an evil force among nations and that defeating Germany was essential to our hopes for a lasting and just world peace. The war was a righteous cause, "a war to end all wars," and we needed to give our complete support to that effort.

Rev. Holmes gave an eloquent and passionate speech denouncing the war. He admitted that there were strong disagreements among us, noting that some felt, like me, that it was necessary to stop Germany. Some supported the war as "the lesser of two evils." Others sought to end the war at any price. And still others, like Rev. Holmes, were pacifists, opposing all violence on moral grounds.

Since there were strong differences about what to do, Rev. Holmes suggested that our Unitarian movement engage in a "ministry of reconciliation," rising above taking sides, and adding our compassion and knowledge to the cause of making a new world without war.

Though I was impressed with his idealism and his vision of the modern church, I thought Rev. Holmes' speech ignored the reality of what was going on in Europe. Our house was on fire, and we had to put out the flames. I proposed a motion that the Unitarian denomination support the United States' war effort, and it passed by a vote of 236 to 9.

After the war, I became Chief Justice of the U.S. Supreme Court. My contribution in that role was greater, I believe, than in my role as President. In the nine years I served, I helped to make the Supreme Court more efficient and just in its handling of important legal questions.

My key message to all people was that our problems have to be solved by improving our existing institutions. High-sounding ideals are useful only when they lead directly to the kind of peace that can be enforced justly.

Unit Four ♦ Looking Back, Moving Ahead

The focus of this unit is a peace and social justice project that the participants begin in Session 10 and conclude in Session 12. This activity encourages the young people to bring together what they have learned and experienced throughout this program and apply this understanding and these feelings and insights to their own lives. It also gives them an opportunity to make a personal commitment to taking action for peace and justice.

Session 10 first engages the young people in reviewing elements of the Unitarian Universalist story and vision relating to peace and social justice. The session then invites the participants to make a commitment to their own peace and justice projects, either individually or in groups, and to begin working on these projects.

In Session 11, participants explore two methods of social change, legal protest and civil disobedience. They also continue to work on their peace and social justice projects.

In Session 12, participants complete their projects and celebrate both their achievement and the conclusion of this program.

Session 10 ◆ Beginning a Peace and Justice Project

Goals for Participants

- to review the Unitarian Universalist story and vision they explored in previous sessions
- to make a commitment to enacting a peace and justice project, to select their project, and to begin work on it.

Overview

In this session participants first review some of what they have learned about the Unitarian Universalist story and vision for peace and justice. Then the session invites them to make a commitment to work on their own peace and justice projects in the context of this program.

It is essential to the value of this experience that the young people perceive this invitation as a genuine one, so that their decision to do a project is a genuine choice on their part. Structure this decision so the majority of the group rules. The most likely scenarios include the following:

- Everyone in the group wants to do a project. With this outcome, you have no problems!

- The majority wants to do projects, but one or a few do not. With this outcome, ask the one or few to go along with the choice of the majority.

- The majority does not want to do projects. With this outcome, omit the projects as an activity and revise this unit accordingly.

Please note that projects can be done individually or in pairs and trios. Prior to this session, consider the skills and characteristics of your participants, and decide if you want to let them choose how to group themselves for the projects, or if you wish to provide guidance in that process.

Materials

- Copies of Handout 7, "Unitarian Universalist Forebears," and Handout 8, "Project Ideas"
- Pens and pencils
- Scratch paper, stationery, envelopes, and stamps
- A writing surface, such as a book, magazine, or clipboard, for each participant
- Markers, paints, and other art media
- Construction paper, tagboard, and newsprint
- Glue, tape, and scissors
- Chalice, candle, and matches

Preparation

- Set up your usual circle.

- Set up the work tables and chairs.

- Review the "Project Ideas" and, if you wish, add ideas to the list before you make copies.

- Consider the guidance you want to give the young people as they choose projects. For the project activity, have one adult as a resource for every five or six participants. If you need to recruit assistants for this project, be sure they know that this involvement is for three sessions. Prior to the session, brief your assistant(s) about the session plan. Give them copies of the handouts, and discuss with them the purpose of the projects, the kinds of projects that are appropriate, and their role as the assistants.

Session Plan

Gathering   8-10 minutes

Greet the young people as they arrive. When the group has gathered, ask people to join you in the circle.

If you have assistants, introduce them to the group and explain their role. Ask people to describe something that happened to them in the past week that surprised them.

When all have shared who wish, engage the young people in playing an active game.

Focusing   10-12 minutes

Gather the participants in your circle. Briefly review what the group has done so far. Note that this session marks the start of the final unit in this program, and give the participants an overview of this session.

Have the young people organize themselves into pairs and trios. Hand out the pencils, writing surfaces, and Handout 7. Ask participants to work in pairs or trios to fill in the blanks with the correct names. Note that this activity reviews some of the stories they have heard about Unitarians and Universalists who contributed to making peace and building justice. Ask them to begin.

When the pairs and trios have finished, gather the group in a circle. Go over these answers:

1. Clara Barton
2. William Howard Taft
3. Benjamin Rush
4. Susan B. Anthony
5. Adin Ballou
6. Horace Mann
7. Mary Livermore
8. John Haynes Holmes
9. Dorothea Dix
10. Theodore Parker
11. Julia Ward Howe

Welcome questions and comments about any of these persons.

Reflecting   4-6 minutes

Ask the participants to consider the following question: "Of the 11 Unitarians and Universalists we have just identified, which person is the most interesting to you, and why?"

Pause for a minute, then invite people to share their responses.

Exploring   8-12 minutes

Explain that you are going to invite the group to work on peace and justice projects, beginning today and concluding in your final session. Tell the young people that it is their decision whether or not to do projects. Explain that the majority of the group will rule in this decision.

Note that you would like them to decide about the projects in a few minutes, but first you would like the group to brainstorm a list of possible projects so they know what their decision is about. Review the rules for brainstorming.

Post a sheet of newsprint, and ask participants to suggest possible project ideas. Write all of the suggested ideas on the newsprint.

When the group has run out of suggestions, distribute Handout 8. Invite people to look over these sheets, and check any ideas that interest them that have not already been suggested. Give participants time to read the lists, then have them share the ideas they have checked. Add new ideas to the brainstorming list.

Now invite the group to make a decision about doing projects. Explain that choosing to do a project involves making an effort to work for peace and justice and that it is important that people be clear that they want to make this commitment. Facilitate discussion as needed, and help the group arrive at a decision. Then respond to the group's decision according to the guidelines in the Overview.

Integrating   15-25 minutes

Ask participants to indicate with a show of hands who wants to work alone and who wants to work in a pair or trio. Then have those who wish to work with others form pairs and trios.

Invite the participants to choose a project. Ask individuals, pairs, and trios to raise their hands when they have made a choice, so they can tell you (or your assistant(s)) what they have chosen. The leaders need to hear all the choices before participants begin to work, so you can be sure that each project selection is appropriate for this context and can be completed in the time available. Then, as time allows, help the young people begin to work on their projects. Make the various materials available. Circulate among the young people, and provide aid and encouragement.

Closing 4-7 minutes

When time requires, have participants clean up. Then have them gather in a circle. Tell people that they will have time during the next two sessions to work on and finish their projects.

Give the group a brief preview of the next session. Then place the chalice in the center of the circle and have a participant light it. Say, "May this flame remind us of the power that we have to contribute to making peace and building justice among the people we know, and in the larger world."

Allow a few moments of silence. If desired, engage the group in singing a song. Then have a participant extinguish the chalice. Say goodbye.

Reflection and Planning

Consider these questions, and discuss them your co-leader(s) and assistant(s):

1. How do I feel about this session?

2. If I were to lead it again, what would I do differently?

3. How do the participants feel about what they are learning about Unitarian Universalism? About peacemaking and justice-building?

4. What preparation do I need to do for the next session?

Session 11 ◆ Exploring Politics and Protest

Goals for Participants

- to explore why people choose to act for social change
- to consider various means of social action, including legal protest and civil disobedience
- to continue to work on their peace and social justice projects.

Overview

The first part of this session introduces participants to some ways that legal protest and civil disobedience have brought about social and political change. The young people explore a variety of historical examples of both legal protest and civil disobedience and consider their reactions to these events. See Preparation for suggestions on presenting these stories to the group.

In this context, the term "legal protest" refers to the range of political activities that are legal but are generally outside the official channels of the political process. These include public speaking, petitions, demonstrations, pickets, boycotts, and strikes. Civil disobedience refers to illegal actions undertaken against authority in a nonviolent way. It involves selective violation of the law as well as the acceptance of the consequences for such action. Civil disobedience is usually a protest against laws considered to be unjust. Examples include refusal to pay taxes or obey court orders.

When people seek to effect change, they usually try to work through the political process first, if that process is open to them. If such attempts fail, they often change tactics to political protest and perhaps to civil disobedience. The actions people take to create change depend on the nature of the issue, the effort that people are prepared to devote to this purpose, and the risk and consequences they are willing to accept. When people feel that fundamental principles are at stake, such as freedom or equality, they are much more likely to consider civil disobedience or even violent action.

Junior high-age youth often have a keen sense of fairness and a strong idealism that can be drawn on to help them appreciate the actions of those who seek to change unjust laws and exploitative social structures. Help participants gain insight into the values and motivations of people who use legal protest and civil disobedience for justice-building and peacemaking.

In the second part of this session, participants continue to work on their projects. If any person or group completes a project, invite that person or group to work on a second project or help others.

Materials

- Copies of Handouts 9-12, four stories
- An audiotape and a tape player
- Materials for the peace and justice projects
- Chalice, candle, and matches

Preparation

- A major activity of this session is hearing and discussing the stories of four individuals who used legal protest and civil disobedience to effect social change. These four stories can be presented most dramatically by recording them on audiotape with the voices of different people within or outside the congregation. Be sure to record a pause between Part 1 and Part 2 of each story. If it is not possible to make a recording, the stories can be read aloud by leaders or participants as descibed in the session plan.

- Set up your usual circle.

- Have work tables and chairs available.

- Be familiar with the four stories.

- If possible, arrange for someone to visit your group and sing "Bread and Roses" (see Index to Music) after the third story.

Session Plan

Gathering   8-10 minutes

Greet the young people as they arrive. When the group has gathered, ask people to join you in the circle.

Ask the participants to share what their peace and justice projects are. Give a brief overview of this session, and then engage the group in playing an active game.

Focusing, Reflecting, and Exploring   18-20 minutes

Begin this activity by saying something like: "When people experience injustice and violence, they often feel compelled to take strong action. Listen to the story of one such action, and see what you think of it."

Play Part 1 of the first story on the story tape. Then discuss with the participants how Gandhi might act in this situation. After a few minutes, play Part 2. Invite comments and questions.

Follow the same procedure with the other stories. If you have arranged for someone to sing "Bread and Roses," plan for this performance to take place after you have completed the third story. Explain that the song was written about this strike. Invite reactions.

Give participants copies of the stories (Handouts 9-12), and invite them to keep them and read them when they wish.

Integrating   4-8 minutes

Involve the young people in a discussion of the following questions if you have not already explored them:

1. Many of these people broke the law. Under what conditions, if any, is it right to do so?

2. Is there any principle of right and wrong that would justify breaking the law?

Project   20-25 minutes

Allow the participants to work on their peace and justice projects.

Closing   4-7 minutes

Have the young people clean up, then gather them in a circle. Give the group a preview of the next session.

Place the chalice in the center of the circle, and have a participant light it. Say, "As Unitarian Universalists we affirm the rights of each person's conscience. May this flame remind us that it takes courage for people to change the world for the better."

Allow a few moments for reflection. If desired, engage the group in singing a song. Then have a participant extinguish the chalice. Say goodbye.

Be aware of how the participants are progressing with their projects. Provide the support they need to complete their projects in the beginning of the next session.

Reflection and Planning

Consider these questions, and discuss them with your co-leader(s):

1. What was the best part of this session? The worst?

2. What can I learn from the experience of this session that can help me to become a better leader for this group?

3. What preparation do I need to do for the next session?

Session 12 ♦ Completing and Celebrating

Goals for Participants

- to complete their peace and justice projects and experience a feeling of accomplishment
- to reflect on their experience in this program
- to celebrate their participation in this program
- to feel a sense of completion.

Overview

In this session the young people complete their projects and celebrate their participation in this program. As well as simply enjoying themselves during the celebration, it is important for them to reflect on their experiences and share a little about this experience with their peers.

Materials

- Rolls of crepe paper of various colors
- Masking tape
- Refreshments
- Chalice, candle, and matches

Preparation

- Set up your usual circle.

- Make arrangements for the refreshments.

Session Plan

Gathering   5-7 minutes

Greet participants as they arrive. When the group has gathered, ask people to join you in the circle. Give participants an overview of this session.

Project   15-25 minutes

Encourage the young people to complete their projects. Have participants who finish early decorate the room with crepe paper. Have people clean up when they complete their projects.

Sharing   10-14 minutes

Gather the group in a circle. Invite participants to share what they have done. Affirm the accomplishments of each participant.

When all have shared about their projects, invite people to reflect on what they have experienced in this program. You may want to review the sessions quickly. Allow a few moments of silence for reflection, then invite participants to share their responses to the following question: "What is something I have learned in this program that is meaningful to me?" When all have shared who wish to, share some of your own discoveries and positive feelings about this group and the experience you have had together.

Celebrating   15-20 minutes

Engage the young people in celebrating their accomplishments with their projects and their participation in this group with games and refreshments.

Closing   4-6 minutes

Gather the group in a circle. Place the chalice in the center of the circle, and have a participant light it. Say, "As Unitarian Universalists, we aspire to peace and justice for all who dwell on this earth. May this flame remind us that it is small steps that can lead to great strides, that each effort for a better world counts."

Allow a few moments of silence, and say, "I'd like to close by sharing with you a quote from Eleanor Roosevelt. She was a woman who worked very hard for justice for all and for peace in the world. Her husband was President Franklin Delano Roosevelt. She said, 'It is not enough to talk about peace. One must believe in it. And it isn't enough to believe in it. One must work at it.' May we all continue to talk about, to believe in, and to work for peace and justice in this world."

Allow a few moments of silence, then lead the group in singing "Shalom Haverim" or a song from the Index to Music. Have a participant extinguish the chalice.

Hand out the folders or envelopes, and invite the young people to take them home and share them with their families. Say goodbye.

Reflection and Planning

Consider these questions, and discuss them with your co-leader(s):

1. How do I feel about this entire program?

2. What have I learned from the experience of leading this program?

3. If I were to start again in a month, what would I do differently?

Evaluation

Please take the time to photocopy the evaluation of *In Our Hands: Junior High* at the end of this program, discuss it with your co-leader(s), and fill it out. Then return it to the Curriculum Office, Department of Religious Education, Unitarian Universalist Association, 25 Beacon St., Boston, MA 02108.

Index to Games

Games

How Do You Do?

Despite the fact that this game involves as mad a scramble as any circular chasing contest, its players never totally abandon their sense of etiquette.

We attend this game as party guests, standing in a circle and facing the center. One of us volunteers to be the host. He walks around the outside of the circle, behind our backs, and selects one player by tapping her on the shoulder. Now the pleasantries begin.

The host shakes the hand of the selected guest, introducing himself and inquiring, ever so solicitously, "How do you do?" She tells him her name and responds to his inquiry in her most genteel manner: "Fine, thank you!" But the host proves to be exceedingly gracious (or perhaps just hard of hearing), for he asks again, "How do you do?" whereupon the guest replies again, "Fine, thank you!" The overly gracious host now asks for a third time, "How do you do?" all the while shaking the guest's hand. When she answers for the third time, "Fine, thank you!" all propriety is finally abandoned and the action begins.

The host dashes around the outside of the circle in the direction he was originally going, while the guest runs in the opposite direction. It's a contest to see who can get back to the starting place—home—first. However, when their paths cross somewhere on the other side of the circle, the host and guest must stop, shake hands again, and go through the formalities three more times: "How do you do?" "Fine thank you!""How do you do?" "Fine thank you!""How do you do?" "Fine thank you!" They then continue on around the circle. Whoever gets beaten in the race home gets to host the party for the next round.

Can we add even more life to this madcap affair? How about specifying different forms of locomotion for the trip around the circle—hopping, skipping, or side-stepping, perhaps. Or how about making the host and the guest get around the circle walking backward or with their eyes closed? Or we could exchange pleasantries and race around the circle in pairs, just to add to the formal frenzy?

Instant Replay

Ever get the feeling that all those spectacular touchdown passes we see over and over on the tube each week are cut from the same piece of film? The instant replays in this game are not only guaranteed to be unique, they also provide a perfect way for us to introduce ourselves—again and again and again.

Let's all stand in a circle, facing each other. One of us starts by moving into the center and announcing his name while performing whatever movements and gestures he chooses. For instance, he might skip into the center and perform a grand sweeping of his hand, proclaiming to all, "Fred!" (assuming that's his name, of course), and then skip back to his place in the circle. That's the signal for everyone else to do exactly as he did, in unison, mimicking him in both deed and word as closely as possible.

Next, its Sarah's turn. Maybe she slithers into the center and hisses a serpentine "Ssssarah!" The rest of us then get to be snakelike too. We proceed around the circle, each of us getting a turn to announce himself in his own may and to see himself in multiple instant replay.

The announcements can convey occupations or secret selves, or they can have no particular meaning at all. With or without categories, the first player can get things rolling in the right spirit by setting a creatively silly example. But everyone else should choose motions that everyone else will be able to repeat; in other words, no two-and-a-half gainers with a slipped disc (also known as the Not Nadia rule).

The best part of this game is there's no such thing as a second-rate performance. If you think you're going to play it safe by timidly trudging into the circle and muttering "Marie," just wait until you see yourself on instant replay.

Rainstorm

One person acts as the conductor of the storm and stands in the center of the circle. As with an orchestra, the conductor brings each person into the storm (symphony) in turn. Standing in front of one person, the conductor starts rubbing his or her own hands together. The person imitates the motion. The conductor turns around slowly in place until everyone is rubbing hands together. Then, coming around to the first person again, and while everyone is still rubbing hands, he or she starts snapping fingers. This motion also goes all the way around, with each person continuing the first motion until getting a new direction from the conductor. The game goes on with hands slapping thighs, and finally with both slapping of thighs and stamping of feet—the crescendo of the storm. As with a thundershower, the volume decreases as the conductor goes through the above steps in reverse order until the last person rubbing hands is silent.

A What?

The name of this game is A What? A What?? A What?! And if that's confusing, just wait until we start playing. In this game, no one ever knows exactly what is happening.

We stand in a circle, facing the center. One of us starts the action by taking a ball (any object will do) and handing it to the person on her right, saying, "This is a banana."

The person who now holds the ball is evidently already confused, because she inquires, "A what??" The first player repeats, "A banana!"

Person number two, her confusion temporarily cleared up, hands the ball to the person on her right and says, "This is a banana." Now person number three is confused. "A what???" he asks of number two. She then turns back to number one and asks again, "A what??" "A banana!" She says. Whereupon number two turns back to three and confirms it, "A banana!!" she says. Now that number three is enlightened, he can hand the ball he's been holding to number four and say, "This is a banana." And when number four asks, "A what????" the whole sequence gets played back to number one: "A what?" "A what??" "A banana!" "A banana!!" "A banana!!!"

While number four starts the process all over again with number five, number one takes another ball, hands it to the person on her left, and says, "This is a pineapple." "A what??" and the pineapple takes off to the left. By the time the two balls collide somewhere in the center, who'll be able to say for sure what's what?

When we become pros as this game, we can add more fruit to the fruit bowl. Maybe a pomegranate. A what?

Name Train

Every player is a superstar in this game, and here's a way to make sure that each of us receives an ovation to match that status.

We stand in a circle, facing the center, and one player volunteers to be the locomotive. If he's a genuine railroad buff, he'll take a few chugs around the circle, piston driving with his arms, choo-chooing, and maybe letting blast with a steam whistle or two. (No diesels in this game.)

The locomotive stops and exchanges introductions with one of us in the circle. "Hi, I'm Bob." "Hello, I'm Mary." Upon learning the person's name, Bob the locomotive breaks into a semaphoric cheer, alternately raising his arms and extending his legs while chanting the person's name, "Mary! Mary! Mary, Mary, Mary!"

After Mary has been hailed, Bob the locomotive turns around, Mary places her hands on his hips as a caboose, and the two of them chug across the circle to find another person to introduce themselves to. "Hi. I'm Gregory," says the chosen player. Bob repeats Gregory's name; then Mary repeats it; and then they both break into a semaphoric euphoria, chanting, "Gregory! Gregory! Gregory, Gregory, Gregory!" Following Gregory's chant, Mary becomes the locomotive, Bob puts his hands on her waist, and Gregory joins the train as the new caboose, and they all chug off to acquire another car.

We continue adding cars to the train, cheering everyone by name as we go along. We might even split into two or more trains (depending on the number of players) before each of us has been duly celebrated.

Killer

This game is a classic whodunit. It seems that there's a sneaky killer operating in our midst. How do we know? We're being bumped off one by one. It's up to all of us to give our best Miss Marple and Hercule Poirot performances and force the villain to confess before we're all wiped out.

We start by assembling a cast of characters for our mystery and selecting the killer. We can choose pieces of paper, one of which is marked with a cross to signify the killer, or we can close our eyes, place our thumbs together, and have someone who is not playing choose the killer by squeezing one set of thumbs. Once we have a killer, it's simply a matter of whether he will murder us all before being caught in the act.

The killer's modus operandi is exceptionally clandestine—a wink of the eye directed at an intended victim does the trick. As the game gets underway, we mingle, exchanging furtive glances. If any of us is winked at, he's just been murdered.

The victim has the opportunity to do his favorite death scene. Since it is important that the whole group knows who has been eliminated, he's encouraged to crumple, stagger, and gasp as part of the dying act. To keep the killer's identity from being too obvious, though, there should be a three-to-five second delay between the wink and the death throes.

For the survivors, the situation is becoming more grim by the moment. Our companions are dropping all around us. We'd better discover the murderer before we, too, are eliminated from the game in a wink. What's our deductive method? If one of us suspects the killer's identity, she says, "I have an accusation." However, a single accusation does not suffice in this game. Unless someone else says, "I second the accusation," we've got to continue playing.

If another suspicious soul does second, the two accusers count to three and point to the player they each think is the perpetrator—no conferences allowed. If they both point to a suspect who's innocent, or if they both point to different suspects (even if one of those suspects is guilty), they're dead on the spot because of inept detective work. If, however, they both point to the true killer, he makes a complete and remorseful confession, and the crime of the century is solved.

Killer provides marvelous opportunities for creative variations, supplemental rules, and devious strategies. In Classic Killer, for example, we don't mingle. Instead we sit in a circle so everyone has a clear view of everyone else while our eyes jump and dart in anticipation of the fatal wink. Marathon Killer, in which we set up the game and then go about our business, is a great game for adding suspense and drama to an evening gathering or weekend event. In Killer Plague, a murdered victim can take others to the grave if he tags them as he dies. In all forms of Killer, beware of the setup or doublecross. What happens if the prime suspect seconds an accusation?

If all this murderous activity is offensive, we can change the fantasy and play Lover, with romantic swoons instead of death throes.

Stand Up

This cooperative game is one of our favorites. You can start with just one friend and end up with a whole crowd of struggling, stumbling, giggling humanity.

Sit on the ground, back to back with your partner, knees bent together and elbows linked. Now simply stand together. With a bit of cooperation and a little practice, this shouldn't be too hard.

By the time you've got this mastered, you'll probably have drawn an interested spectator. Have this person join you on the ground, and all three try to stand up. The feat should take you just long enough to attract another onlooker. Have him join you. Four people standing up together might be a genuine accomplishment.

By this time, you should realize that there's more struggling, stumbling, and giggling each time you add another person. But this very fact assures you of an endless supply of fascinated spectators, ready to join up to help you get off the ground.

A gracefully executed Mass Stand Up (any number greater than five) is like a blossoming flower—but a more rare event. To achieve it, start by sitting close and firmly packed. Then all stand up quickly and at precisely the same moment.

Judging by the records, it must be easier to go down than up. Can you imagine 1,468 champion Lap Sitters in Palos Verdes playing Stand Up together? However, we're confident that somewhere a group of dedicated gymnasts is practicing for the World Stand Up Record. Write us if you think you and your friends have made it.

Red-Handed

Here's a legitimate chance to see how sneaky you can be. And the only consequence if you get caught is having to catch someone who might be even sneakier.

Everyone forms a circle, and one person, chosen as IT, stands in the center. While IT closes her eyes, the other players pass a small object (like a marble or a stone) from person to person.

The sneakiest method of passing is to hold the marble in one fist, palm down, and drop it in the palm-up hand of the next person. Then he passes it from one fist to the other and so on. With a little practice, you'll be able to accomplish a quick and sneaky pass without even looking.

IT signals and opens her eyes. Who among all these innocent-looking people has the marble? If she detects a suspicious look on someone's face, she walks up and taps one of his fists. If he's empty-handed, she moves on. Meanwhile everyone has been passing the marble around, virtually under IT's nose. (Fake passes, as decoys, by people who don't have the marble are an integral part of the game.)

If you have the marble and IT catches your eye, she may soon catch more than that unless you can pull a good angel face. If she sees through that to the sneaky devil beneath, you've been caught "Red-Handed." Congratulations! You're the new IT.

Animal Sounds

Room darkened; eyes closed; one large ball. Everyone sits in a circle and people in turn select and mimic different animal sounds as their own personal signals. The initiator of the game makes her or his sound and then the sound of the "animal" to which he or she intended to roll the ball. The "animal" whose sound is made replies (to help initiator direct the ball). The initiator then rolls the ball toward the intended animal. If that animal receives the ball, he or she responds with her or his sound and the animals show happiness by making all their sounds in unison (this also reminds others what animals are present.). If the initiator misses the intended animal, the animal that receives the ball returns it to the initiator after making her or his sound.

Barnyard

People stand in a large circle, choose six animals (fewer for a group smaller than 20) and count off by animals; or a slip of paper with the name of an animal on it is passed out to each person. Then, with everyone's eyes closed (or a dark room could be used), each person finds all the others of his or her kind by constantly calling the animal sounds, "Baa-a-a," "Meow, meow," etc. When two of the same animals cross each other, they hold hands and find others until they are all together. It is a very funny game. Note: The idea is not to finish first, but merely to find your own kind.

Dragon

Works best with no more than seven adults, or no more than seven or eight children. Everyone gets into a line holding the waist of the person in front. Then the "head" (first person in line) tries to touch the "tail" (last person in line) while the "body" (people in between) help the "tail" from being touched without anyone losing grip of the waist of the person in front. If there is more than one line, then each line can operate independently of each other or think up something that would cause the various lines to interact.

Pru-ee

A delightful activity for large groups (15 or more). All eyes should be closed. The leader whispers in someone's ear "You're the PRU-EE." Now everyone, including the PRU-EE, begins to mingle with eyes shut. Each person is to find another's hand, shake it, and ask, "Pru-ee?" If the other person also asks "Pru-ee?" they drop hands and go on to someone else. Everyone goes around asking except the PRU-EE, who remains silent the whole time. When a person gets no response to the question "Pru-ee?" he or she knows that the PRU-EE is found, hangs onto that hand, and becomes part of PRU-EE, also remaining silent. Anyone shaking hands with PRU-EE (now two people) becomes part of it, making it larger and larger. If someone finds only clasped hands and silence, he or she can join the line at that point. Soon the cries of "Pru-ee?" will dwindle, and the PRU-EE will increase until everyone in the room is holding hands. Then the leader asks for eyes to be opened. There are always gasps of surprise and laughter. Note: The "pru-ee?" sounds like a high-pitched bird call.

Knots

Everyone closes eyes and moves together, each person taking another person's hands in each of his or her own hands. When each person has two hands, then all open their eyes and try to untangle themselves without dropping hands. The group must work together to get out the knots. It leads to very amusing situations, because although the group may end up in one big circle, most of the time there will be a knot or two in the circle, and even two or more circles, either intertwined or separate. It's great fun and leads to group cooperation.

Clapping Game

One person goes out of the room. The rest of the group decides on an object for the person to find, or an action for the person to do. The person returns to try to find the object while the group claps. The group will help the person complete the task by clapping louder and louder as the person approaches the object or starts to discover the act decided upon. If the person is not catching on, the clapping is soft.

Variation: This game can also be played with two people going out of the room and coming back to do something in tandem. Examples of things to have people do together: hug each other, face each other with hands on shoulders, sit back-to-back. Think up your own variations.

Index to Music

Bread and Roses

Words by James Oppenheim

Music by Caroline Kohlsaat

May The Light Of The Spirit Surround You

Listen, Listen, Listen!

Happiness Flows

Hap-pi-ness flows in a cir-cu-lar mo-tion. Love is like a lit-tle boat up - on the sea.

Ev-'ry-bod-y is a part of ev-'ry-thing an-y-way. You can have it all if you let yourself be.

REFRAIN

Hap-pi-ness flows, hap-pi-ness flows, hap-pi-ness flows, hap-pi-ness flows.

Dear Friends

Variation:
Dear friends and family,
How can I show you how I feel?
You have filled my life with meaning,
And I love you so.

May The Long Time Sun Shine Upon You

Treasure Hunt

In the spaces below, write the names of people who fit the description given. Try to get the name of every person in the room listed in a space. (You don't need to fill every space, though!)

1. People who wonder what they want to do when they grow up.

2. People who see themselves more as a "funnybone" than a "backbone."

3. People who have helped someone else in the past two weeks.

4. People who have had a good laugh in the last week.

5. People who like _____ .

6. People who see themselves as creative.

7. People who like math.

8. People who like music.

9. People who have someone in their family who has taken part in a peace march.

10. People who have read a newspaper recently.

11. People who know what the letters UUSC stand for.

Hunger–A World Divided

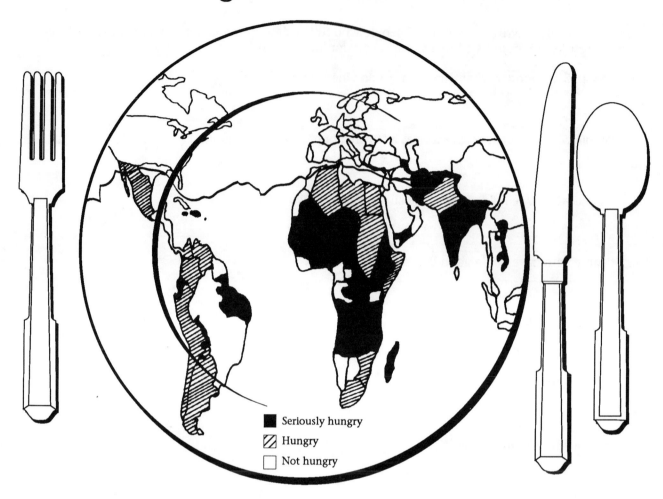

Seriously hungry

Hungry

Not hungry

The crack in the plate represents the division between the North and the South — the rich and the poor nations of our world.

1. Approximately_____people, or 25% of the world's population, are chronically malnourished.
    a. 100 million   b. 500 million c. 750 million d. One billion

2. More than_____deaths each year result from hunger and starvation.
    a. 150,000 b. 800,000   c. 3,000,000   d. 13,000,000

3. Of this number,_____are children.
    a. 1/4   b. 1/3 c. 1/2 d. 3/4

4. People who live south of the North-South dividing line represent 70% of the world's population and possess_____% of the world's income.
    a. 8   b. 17   c. 40   d. 50

5   The average life span of a person in the North is more than 70 years. In the South the average is years.
    a. 35   b. 45 c. 50   d. 65

6. In the 83 poorest countries of the South,_____% of the people control 80% of the land.
    a. 3   b. 13   c. 23   d. 43

From an activity produced by Church World Service, P. O. Box 968, Elkhart, IN.

Reflection Questions–A

1. Do you know people who refuse to fight as a matter of principle?

2. What are some good reasons to oppose all violence?

3. What are some good reasons to use violent force?

Reflection Questions–B

1. What are some good things about our country that would be worth fighting for?

2. Should people defend their country "right or wrong"?

Definitions

Self-interest: Concern with meeting one's own needs or pursuing one's own values. This term can be applied to individuals, groups, or nations.

Militarist: One who prefers military solutions to problems between nations rather than negotiation or talking things over.

Pacifist: One who insists on peaceful solutions to all problems and refuses to participate in military efforts.

Nonviolent Resistance: A lifestyle of confronting injustice and attempting to eliminate it without using physical force or violence in any way.

Nationalist: One who favors the interests of his or her country above the interests of other countries.

Internationalist: One who favors the collective interests of all peoples over the interests of any single nation.

Unitarian Universalist Principles

We believe in the following principles, and we join together to support them.

- We believe that each and every person is important.

- We believe that all people deserve to be treated with fairness and kindness.

- We believe that our churches and fellowships should be places where people accept each other and where we can learn and grow together.

- We believe that each person must be free to search for what is right and true in life.

- We believe that each person must be guided by her or his conscience, and that people should have a say in decisions that affect them.

- We believe in working for a peaceful, fair, and free world.

- We believe in caring for and taking care of our planet Earth.

Unitarian Universalist Forebears

Dorothea Dix (1802-87)   Horace Mann (1796-1859)

Benjamin Rush (1745-1813)   Julia Ward Howe (1819-1910)

Theodore Parker (1810-60)   Adin Ballou (1803-90)

Susan B. Anthony (1820-1906)   Mary Livermore (1820-1905)

Clara Barton (1821-1912)   John Haynes Holmes (1879-1964)

William Howard Taft (1857-1930)

Who am I? *Fill in the blank with the correct name.*

1. _____ I am a Universalist who helped found the American Chapter of the Red Cross.

2. _____ I am a Unitarian who criticized pacifism and advocated ensuring peace by having strong institutions.

3. _____ I am a Universalist who worked as a reformer during the U. S. Revolution and signed the Declaration of Independence.

4. _____ I am a Unitarian who saw nothing in the U.S. Constitution that prevented women from voting.

5. _____ I am a Universalist pacifist who established an experimental community to live by the law of love.

6. _____ I am a Unitarian who worked to create a system of public education for children from all backgrounds.

7. _____ I am a Universalist suffragist and writer who helped to give humanitarian aid to both sides in the U.S. Civil War.

8. _____ I am a Unitarian minister who advocated pacifism during both World Wars.

9. _____ I am a Unitarian who helped to reform prisons and institutions for the mentally ill.

10. _____ I am a Unitarian who strongly opposed slavery and believed that "permanent truth" will outlast Christianity.

11. _____ I am a Unitarian who opposed slavery and later played a role in the struggles for women's rights and world peace.

Project Ideas

For Individuals

- Design a peace/justice bumper sticker.
- Design a peace/justice banner or poster.
- Design a new peace/justice symbol.
- Design a world peace flag.
- Design a peace/justice ad for your next church/fellowship newsletter.
- Write an article for the newsletter about peace/justice.
- Write a letter to your local newspaper about a peace/justice issue.
- Write a letter to your local representative or to the Prime Minister or President about a peace/justice issue.
- Write a letter to the General Secretary of the Communist Party of the Soviet Union about a peace/justice issue.
- Start a petition about a peace/justice issue, and collect signatures.

For Individuals or Groups

- Write and sign a peace/justice pledge.
- Make and distribute peace/justice buttons.
- Make a piece of artwork for a junior high class in the Soviet Union about peace/justice, and send it to the class.
- Write a peace/justice letter to: someone you are afraid of; someone who you think is acting unfairly; the mayor of your town; a student in the Soviet Union; the leader of another country.

For Groups

- Organize a clothes/toys collection for a service organization such as Goodwill.
- Organize a food collection for a local hunger project.
- Prepare and/or serve food at a local program that serves meals to those in need.
- Set up a donation table for a peace/justice project or organization.
- Organize a peace/justice forum, debate, or study group.
- Set up a peace/justice pamphlet and book library in your congregation.

Gandhi and the Salt March

Part 1

My name is Mohandas K. Gandhi. My people call me "Mahatma," meaning "great soul." I am the leader of the struggle for the people of India to gain their independence from British rule. It is now 1930, and I am 61 years old. For the past 10 years I have tried to get the British to grant us freedom, so far without much success. We Indians vastly outnumber the British, yet they have almost total control of our lives. I am sure that freedom would be ours if we could just take it. But I am also committed to nonviolence. How can I mobilize my own people and convince the British to leave India without bloodshed? I am running out of ideas.

The British humiliate us with their laws. Why, they have a monopoly on salt, which they tax highly and sell to us. There it lies on the seashore, a gift of God, and yet we are forbidden to take it. We have to buy it from them. I wrote a letter to the British Viceroy protesting this situation. In the letter I complained of the unjust Salt Laws and pledged to engage in nonviolent civil disobedience, not merely to have the laws repealed, but to force the British to leave. He wrote back, warning me against disobeying the law.

My people are looking to me for leadership. I need their support and the strength of their numbers. Everyone is wondering, what will I do? Thousands of people have surrounded my village and are waiting for me to act. What shall I do next?

Part 2

Mahatma Gandhi led a march from his village to the sea, 240 miles away. Along the way, thousands of people joined the procession. When they reached the seashore, Gandhi said, "Watch, I am about to give a signal to the nation." And then he picked up a handful of salt in defiance of British rule. After that, tens of thousands of Indians up and down India's long seacoast began to make salt from the sea. The British authorities responded with mass arrests. More than 100,000 people were jailed. The British also arrested Gandhi, who was imprisoned without trial. Although the British beat and sometimes shot the protesters, the Indian people did not resort to violence.

As a result of Gandhi's march to the sea, India won its independence, not politically—that would not happen for another 17 years — but morally. Gandhi and his followers made the British people aware that they were ruling India in a cruel way. More importantly, the Salt March gave the Indian people the conviction that they could throw off the British if they simply refused to be ruled.

Rosa Parks
and the Montgomery Bus Boycott

Part 1

My name is Rosa Parks. I live in Montgomery, Alabama. Since I was a young girl, I have had to live by unfair rules just because I am a black person. I couldn't go to the same school as white kids. Theirs was big and new. Mine was a one-room shack. I couldn't drink from the same water fountains, eat at the same restaurants, use the same bathrooms, or go to the same movie theaters.

When I ride on a bus, I am required to sit in back, because the front seats are reserved for whites. And when there aren't enough seats for white folks, the driver makes the black people give up their seats and stand. If blacks refuse to do this, they can be put in jail, because that's what the law says here in Montgomery in 1955.

My mother said to me, "Be proud of yourself. Be proud of black people." And so, even after working hard all day as a seamstress, I counsel young people and teach adults to pass the voting test. But it troubles me to see my people treated so unfairly.

Today has been a hard day. Too tired to walk home, I decided to take the bus. Luckily, there was a seat when I got on. But now the bus is filling up with white passengers, and the driver is telling me that I must give up my seat and stand. What can I do?

Part 2

Rosa Parks refused to give up her seat. She was arrested and taken to jail. Other blacks were angered by what had happened to Miss Parks. A group of citizens, including Dr. Martin Luther King, Jr., organized a boycott of Montgomery's buses. Black people started walking to work instead of riding. Some shared rides in cars and vans, but no black people rode the buses.

Rosa Parks received many threats against her life, but she continued to give speeches about the boycott. Later she was arrested again, along with a hundred other leaders of the black community, including Dr. King. Still the boycott continued. It lasted for 381 days, more than a year. Not until the Supreme Court of the United States ordered the bus company to let black people sit wherever they wanted on buses did the people give up the boycott. Rosa Parks and her fellow citizens had won a victory for justice, without violence.

Bread and Roses:
The Lawrence Textile Strike

Part 1

We are the textile workers of Lawrence, Massachusetts, the biggest producer of wool and cotton cloth in the world. In this year of 1912, there are about 30 thousand of us working in the mills here. We represent 30 different nationalities and speak 50 different languages. Most of us are recent immigrants to the United States from such countries as Italy, Greece, Russia, Poland, and Syria.

Although the mills make a very good profit, we are paid starvation wages. We earn between $6.00 and $7.50 a week. That makes $300 to $400 a year. This is well below the poverty level, even in 1912. For us to survive, as many members of the family as possible have to work. This includes mothers and children. In fact, half of the women and children in Lawrence work in the mills, and they earn much less money than the men.

Half of the deaths in Lawrence each year are children under six years of age. One-third of all people working in the mills die before the age of 25. The working conditions in the mills are unhealthy and dangerous, and the workers are all exploited by the men who own the mills. We live in crowded tenements. We are always hungry. And even though we produce more wool than any other city in the world, we can't afford coats to keep us warm in the winter.

We have just received a cut in our wages and are told that we have to work even harder. What shall we do?

Part 2

On January 12, 1912, the textile workers, led by a group of Polish women, went on strike. By the next day, the ranks of the strikers had grown to 20,000. Using picket lines, they shut down the mills. The strikers, including women and children, protested the low pay and terrible working conditions. Police and militia were sent in to break the strike by attacking the striking workers, including the women and children. Many were arrested, and at least one striker, a woman, was shot and killed by the police.

Despite terrible hardship, the workers stuck together through the harsh winter of 1912. Even though tempers ran high, the workers remained nonviolent in their protest. The strike finally ended on March 14 when the owners agreed to give concessions to the strikers, including a pay increase.

It was called the "Bread and Roses Strike" because of a popular slogan of the strikers: "We want bread and roses, too."

Linus Pauling
and the Nobel Peace Prize

Part 1

I am Dr. Linus Pauling. As a scientist, I received the Nobel Prize for Chemistry in 1954. Since the United States dropped the first atomic bomb on Hiroshima in 1945, I have been concerned about the effects of nuclear radiation. I joined Albert Einstein's committee of scientists who had banded together to speak out against nuclear weapons. But the committee was not strong enough to withstand the pressures of those who wanted to build more bombs because they were afraid of the Russians. A lot of the pressure came from Senator Joseph McCarthy, who attacked many people who wanted peace by calling them communists or traitors.

After working with the committee of scientists, I went on alone, speaking and writing to express my concern about exposure to radiation from nuclear weapons testing and my desire for nuclear disarmament and peace. Because of my pacifist views, however, many people questioned my loyalty to the United States. Some have called me a communist. Even the U.S. State Department considers me a troublemaker and has refused to let me travel outside of the country. What else can I do?

Part 2

Dr. Pauling decided to circulate a petition among his colleagues in science. This petition called for a halt to the testing of nuclear weapons. He gathered signatures from more than 11,000 scientists from all over the world, and presented the petition to the United Nations in 1958. Angered by this petition, some U.S. officials demanded to know the names of all those who had helped Pauling circulate the petition. When Pauling refused to cooperate, these officials threatened to have Pauling imprisoned for a year. There was pressure to have him removed from his teaching position. But Linus Pauling persisted in expressing his views.

In 1963 Dr. Pauling was awarded a second Nobel Prize, this time the Peace Prize, for work he had done on behalf of the above-ground nuclear test ban treaty, which was signed that year by the U.S. and the U.S.S.R. Dr. Pauling is the only person ever to win two unshared Nobel Prizes. He now lives in Santa Barbara, California, where he is a member of the local Unitarian Universalist church.

Evaluation of *In Our Hands: Junior High*

We need you! Help us serve you by sending us your comments, suggestions, and critiques of this program. Please photocopy this form, using additional sheets if needed, and send to: Curriculum Development Office, Unitarian Universalist Association, 25 Beacon Street, Boston, MA 02108-2800.

General Information

1. With what age group did you use this curriculum?

2. Approximately how many participants?

3. How many leaders?

4. Anything else you would like to tell us about your religious education setting (very small or very large congregation, etc.)?

General Comments

Include comments on what worked, what didn't, and how you modified the program to fit your needs.

Comments on Sessions

Session 1: "The Best of All Possible Worlds"

Session 2: Building a Utopian Society

Session 3: Promoting Our Utopian Society

Session 4: What About Prejudice and "-Isms"?

Session 5: What About Hunger and Poverty?

Session 6: What About War and Peace?

Session 7: The Unitarian Universalist Story and Vision

Session 8: A Closer Look

Session 9: Hearing from Our Own

Optional Session: A Meeting of the Minds

Session 10: Beginning a Peace and Justice Project

Session 11: Exploring Politics and Protest

Session 12: Completing and Celebrating